Praise for
Bridge of Courage

"The book is moving, not because of the silent suffering of guerrillas and the oldest genocide in the hemisphere, but because of the unyielding courage and enduring spirit of the Mayan Indians to be free to live in a just society."

—Choice

"Compelling..."

—San Francisco Chronicle

"Read this book...to understand something of the living, breathing flesh-and-blood people who commit their lives to the struggle for liberty."

—Dayton Voice

Extraordinary—heartening accounts of unimaginable bravery and faith..."

—Coleman McCarthy,
Washington Post

"These testimonies are the best expression of the resistance and struggle of a whole people against the brutality of those power structures that refuse to accept the most basic respect for human rights."

—Daniel Ortega, FSLN

"A clear and passionate account of how people who live in fear for their lives and the extinction of their communities can move past the paralysis of fear to unite, form coalitions, share knowledge and courage to fight for their survival. *Bridge of Courage* goes deep into the essence of the Guatemalan people, a people whose courage and tenacity is a lesson of love for us all."

—Winona LaDuke

"The reports of refugees and of the human rights activists who have somehow continued their work under atrocious conditions have provided a gruesome record of what has been happening in these terrible years. The shameful picture is extended in the personal testimonies of the compañeros and compañeras who, with awesome heroism that even their unassuming simplicity cannot disguise, turned to resistance against unending barbarism. As the picture comes to light, a sane person cannot fail to feel outrage and anger, despair that the human soul can harbor such depths of depravity."

—Noam Chomsky, from the Introduction

"If we are to understand our neighbors below the border, their vision and hopes, this is the book to read."

—Studs Terkel

"Must reading for anyone interested in humanity's perpetual struggle against tyranny and oppression."

—William Kunstler

"For those who want to know what makes people give up 'everything' and fight for justice—everywhere."

—Margaret Randall

"Extraordinary... a revolution brought down to the most elemental, human level—terrifying yet inspiring. I wish that every American could read this—it would be a monumental lesson, and perhaps stir a demand that the United States finally act with decency in Latin America."

—Howard Zinn

"Superb...truly essential reading for anyone concerned with the realities of this little-known but ongoing holocaust, and the continuing complicity of the U.S. in perpetrating it."

—Ward Churchill

"This book is everything the publishers claim—it is full of tales of unimaginable courage and hardship and the triumph of the human spirit. It also makes at least this American liberal feel like a hopeless sissy. God knows whether any of us in this country who think we value freedom would have half the strength and commitment these "ordinary people", interviewed by Jennifer Harbury, have shown so consistently. I doubt I could measure up to any of them, but I am comforted by their wisdom. As one woman guerrilla told Harbury, 'you must never laugh at beginners.'"

—Molly Ivins

The weaving on the cover was a gift from Guatemalan villagers to Gaspar Ilom, one of the four commanders of the Guatemalan National Revolutionary Unity (URNG). The translation from the Mayan reads:

Compañero Comandante Gaspar Ilom,
Greetings and Embraces
Merry Christmas and Happy New Year 1990
Success and Triumph
URNG

Bridge of Courage

Life Stories
of the
Guatemalan
Compañeros and Compañeras

Jennifer Harbury

Common Courage Press   Monroe, Maine

Library of Congress Cataloging in Publication Data
from the first edition:

Harbury, Jennifer
Bridge of courage : life stories of the Guatemalan com-
pañeros and compañeras / Jennnifer Harbury.
p. cm
ISBN 1-56751-016-7 (pbk.) -- ISBN 1-56751-01705
(cloth.)
1. Guatemala--History--1945-1985. 2. Guatemala--
History--1985- 3. Unidad Revolucionaria Nacional
Guatemalteca. 4. Government, Resistance to--Guatemala-
-History. 5. Political persecution--Guatemala--History. 6.
Oral history. I. Title.   F1466.5.H3 1994
972.8105'2--dc20   93-19685   CIP

Updated edition ISBN 1-56751-068-x, paper
Updated edition ISBN 1-56751-069-8 cloth

Common Courage Press
P.O. Box 702
Monroe, ME 04951
207-525-0900
Fax: 525-3068

First printing of the updated edition.
First published in 1994.

Dedication

To Everardo
and to all the other
compañeros and compañeras,
alive or fallen,
who have given their lives
to building the bridge.

Contents

Part One: Heeding the Call to Action

Part Two: Life in the Revolution

Part Three: The New Generation

Acknowledgements

I would like to thank the Guatemalan compañeros and compañeras for giving me their time and trust, and the inspiration to write this book. My particular and heart-felt thanks go to Gaspar Ilom, who had the courage to send me to the mountains. Were it not for his decision, the book would not exist, and Everardo would be but a name to me.

It was Deborah, my dear friend of twenty years, who shared her wisdom and writing skills with me. It was only through her bright talents and clarity that the idea for the book began to take form.

It is thanks to Emily Jones and Chris Williams that the book reached publication. I finished writing it the week that Everardo, my husband, disappeared in combat. During the frantic year that followed, it was Emily and Chris who remembered the manuscript, dusted it off, fixed the spacing and the typos and the innumerable spelling errors, and stubbornly sought a publisher. They kept the book alive when I had quite forgotton about it.

I also want to express my love and thanks to Alma, Victor, Robert, Bonnie, Kim and Sam, Emiliano, Rico, Dan, George Max, Alice, Mike, Emma, John and Jane, Lee, Zeke, and Penny. They gave me the confidence and strength to write the book, and kept me going with their optimism , energy, and love. Abrazos fuertes.

Lastly, I want to thank Flic Shooter and Greg Bates of Common Courage Press not only for their belief in this book, (which was far from universal) but for their extraordinary support of our efforts to free Everardo and the other thirty prisoners. They are so very much more than publishers. They are very much more than friends. They are part of the struggle.

GUATEMALA

Mexico

Belize

Mexico

• Tikal

EL PETÉN

Flores

• San Francisco

Gulf of Honduras

Livingston •

• Puerto Barrios

Sebol •

EL QUICHÉ

ALTA VERAPAZ

IZABAL

San Mateo Ixtatán •

Cahabón •

San Miguel Acatán •
Soloma •

HUEHUETENANGO

Chajul •
San Juan
Cotzal •
Cunén •

San
Cristóbal

Cobán

Panzós •

Ixtahuacán • Todos Santos

Nebaj

Pancajche •

• Sacapulas

Uspantán

BAJA VERAPAZ

• San Pedro
Jocopilas

Rabinal

SAN MARCOS

TOTONICAPÁN

Chichicastenango •

San Miguel •
Chicaj

Salamá •

ZACAPA

San Marcos •

San
Cristóbal

El Tumbador •

QUEZALTENANGO

SOLOLA

Cóngora

Jalapa

San
Martín
Jilotepeque

EL PROGRESO

San Luis
Jilotepeque •

Chiquimula •

San Pedro
La Laguna •

Tecpán

Guatemala
City ★

CHIQUIMULA

RETALHULEU

Santiago •

Atitlán

CHIMALTENANGO

SACATEPÉQUEZ

GUATEMALA

JALAPA

• Jalapa

Esquipulas •

SUCHITEPÉQUEZ

• Santa Lucía
Cotzumalguapa

Cuilapa •

Honduras

ESQUINTLA

SANTA ROSA

JUTIAPA

Pacific

Ocean

Iztapa •

San José •

El Salvador

Introduction

"People turn to armed struggle when they do not see an alternative. Of all the people I have known who went down that path, none did so because they wanted it. They didn't spend time debating the ethics of it because to them it was obvious. Ending violence means resolving the situation which gives rise to it."

These remarks were made by Rubén Zamora, the courageous Salvadoran democrat, speaking in Northern Ireland in September 1992. Nowhere are his words more apt than Guatemala, whose rulers for the past 40 years could comfortably rub shoulders with Himmler and Mengele. Commenting in 1990 on the "velvet revolution" in Czechoslovakia, Guatemalan journalist Julio Godoy—who had fled his country a year earlier when his recently reopened newspaper was blown up by state terrorists—observed that Eastern Europeans are, "in a way, luckier than Central Americans":

> While the Moscow-imposed government in Prague would degrade and humiliate reformers, the Washington-made government in Guatemala would kill them. It still does, in a virtual genocide that has taken more than 150,000 victims... [in what Amnesty International calls] a "government program of political murder."

That, he suggested, is "the main explanation for the fearless character of the students' recent uprising in Prague: the Czechoslovak Army doesn't shoot to kill... In Guatemala, not to mention El Salvador, random terror is used to keep unions and peasant associations from seeking their own way." There is an "important difference in the nature of the armies and of their foreign tutors." In the Soviet satellites, the armies were "apolitical and obedient to their national government," while in the U.S. satellites, "the army is the power," doing what they have been trained to do for many decades by their foreign tutor and its client states. "One is tempted to believe that some people in the White House worship Aztec gods—with the offering of Central American blood." They have created and backed forces in El Salvador, Guatemala, and Nicaragua that "can easily compete against Nicolae Ceausescu's Securitate for the World Cruelty Prize."[1]

Guatemala had long endured the "culture of fear" imposed by the military and oligarchy. During the years of FDR's "Good Neighbor Policy," the lash was held by Jorge Ubico, a brutal and murderous dictator whose advent to the Presidency in 1931 was heartily welcomed by the U.S. embassy, concerned, as was the Guatemalan elite, by "a great deal of unrest among the working classes." Ubico legalized the (conventional) murder of Indians by landowners, destroyed the union movement and proscribed mention of such phrases as "trade union" or "labor rights," eliminated any shreds of democracy, and created a highly efficient system of repression and control based on what a U.S. official called his "Guatemalan Gestapo." He was, however, very gracious to U.S. corporations and offered a leading role to U.S. military officers. His frank admiration for Hitler and Mussolini aroused some concerns in the late 1930s, but generally "the American press displayed warm appreciation for Jorge Ubico," historian Piero Gleijeses observes, while the

Roosevelt administration maintained its "stead-fast...approval" for the dictator until the last months of his rule, backing away as he began to lose control—the standard pattern, routinely offering the occasion for odes to our love for democracy and human rights.[2]

The grip of the "culture of fear" was finally broken in 1944, when the dictatorship was overthrown and the country entered a decade of democracy and social progress. "A new wind was stirring the Guatemalan countryside," Gleijeses writes: "The culture of fear was loosening its grip over the great masses of the Guatemalan population. In a not unreachable future, it might have faded away, a distant nightmare." Under President Jacobo Arbenz's agrarian reform, half a million people received desperately needed land, the first time in the history of the country that "the Indians were offered land, rather than being robbed of it."[3]

The awakening from the nightmare in Guatemala aroused the "culture of fear" in Washington. In 1949, the CIA reported "two areas of instability" in Latin America, Bolivia and Guatemala, both threatened by regimes that showed concern for the overwhelming majority of their populations. The CIA elaborated on Guatemalan "instability" in a 1952 report, warning that the "radical and nationalist policies" of the government had gained "the support or acquiescence of almost all Guatemalans." Worse yet, the government was proceeding "to mobilize the hitherto politically inert peasantry" and to create "mass support for the present regime." The government was attaining these goals by labor organization, agrarian and other social reform, and nationalist policies "identified with the Guatemalan revolution of 1944." The revolution had aroused "a strong national movement to free Guatemala from the military dictatorship, social backwardness, and 'economic colonialism' which had been the pattern of the past"; it "inspired the loyalty and conformed to the self-interest of most politically conscious Guatemalans." The democratic programs of the government offered the public a means to participate in achieving these goals, which ran directly counter to the interests of the oligarchy and U.S. agribusiness.

The irresoluble conflict between the goals of the democratic revolution and U.S. policies was spelled out with great clarity by the National Security Council immediately after a CIA coup had destroyed Guatemalan democracy, imposing a reign of terror that far surpassed the achievements of Washington's friend Ubico.[4] The major threat to U.S. interests, the nation's top planning body explained, is posed by "nationalistic regimes" that are responsive to popular pressures for "immediate improvement in the low living standards of the masses" and diversification of their economies. This tendency conflicts not only with the need to "protect our resources" (as George Kennan put it, referring to what is rightfully ours though by irrelevant accident beyond our borders), but also with our concern to encourage "a climate conducive to private investment" and "in the case of foreign capital to repatriate a reasonable return." The Kennedy administration later identified the roots of U.S. interests in Latin America as in part military (the Panama canal, strategic raw materials, etc.), but perhaps still more

"the economic root whose central fiber is the $9 bil-
lion of private U.S. investment in the area" and
extensive trade relations. The need "to protect and
promote American investment and trade," the NSC
continued, is threatened by nationalism; that is,
efforts to follow an independent course. The U.S.
prefers agroexport models serving the interests of
U.S.-based corporations (agribusiness, pesticide
and fertilizer producers, and so on), and in later
years, assembly plants that can provide U.S.
investors with cheap labor, requiring a repressive
climate. "Economic science" is always at hand to
demonstrate that whatever doctrines happen to
benefit Western power are just those that will eventually contribute to the welfare of the subject population—"eventually" referring to "the long run,"
when we are all dead, as Keynes famously put it.
This miraculous coincidence between the conclusions of "economic science" and the self-interest of
the wealthy and powerful arouses no more attention
than the regular refutation of the theories, from the
days of the British in Bengal, Ireland, and elsewhere
until the catastrophe of capitalism that devastated
traditional colonial domains of the West in the
1980s, and is now having the familiar effects in
Eastern Europe, much of it at last returned to its
former quasi-colonial status.

The guiding doctrines of U.S. policy have never
been popular among the targeted populations, a
sign, perhaps, of the "low level of intellectualism"
deplored by the CIA in observations to which we
return. The confrontation in Latin America came to
a head as World War II was ending and the U.S. was
proceeding to establish the rules of the new world

order it intended to dominate. Each region had its place. The Third World generally was reassigned to its traditional service role, each region serving its specific "function." Latin America was to be taken over by the United States, its rivals Britain and France expelled.

At the Chapultepec (Mexico) hemispheric conference in February 1945, Washington called for "An Economic Charter of the Americas" that would eliminate economic nationalism "in all its forms." Latin America, in contrast, upheld "The philosophy of the New Nationalism," as a State Department officer termed it, a policy that "embraces policies designed to bring about a broader distribution of wealth and to raise the standard of living of the masses." State Department Political Adviser Laurence Duggan wrote that

> Economic nationalism is the common denominator of the new aspirations for industrialization. Latin Americans are convinced that the first beneficiaries of the development of a country's resources should be the people of that country.

That curious idea won few accolades in Washington, where it was understood that the "first beneficiaries" should be U.S. investors. Latin America is to complement the needs of the U.S. economy—or more accurately, those who control it—in accordance with the principles of economic science. Accordingly, Latin America should not undergo what the Truman and Eisenhower administrations called "excessive industrial development," meaning development that infringes on the interests of U.S. investors (development that might compete with foreign capital was not deemed "excessive," therefore allowed). Given the power relations, the U.S. position prevailed, with predictable consequences for the region generally.

In this context, one can understand the threat of Guatemalan democracy with its stubborn commitment to the heresy that "the first beneficiaries of the development of a country's resources should be the people of that country." Plainly, such ideas and those who espoused them had no place in the emerging new world order.

Still more ominous was the threat that Guatemalan "instability" might "destabilize" others, who might be impressed by what the democratic reforms were achieving. Guatemala could become what U.S. planners call a "rotten apple" that will "spoil the barrel," a "virus infecting others," a "domino" that might "topple the row." In May 1953, a senior Pentagon official, General Richard Partridge, reported that the "drastic reforms which [Arbenz] is implementing do affect the neighboring countries which are only slightly less overdue for reforms of a similar nature. That explains the great concern of the neighboring countries over his activities." A few months later, as the U.S. campaign to eradicate the virus was in progress, a State Department official warned that Guatemala

> has become an increasing threat to the stability of Honduras and El Salvador. Its agrarian reform is a powerful propaganda weapon; its broad social program of aiding the workers and peasants in a victorious struggle against the upper classes and large foreign enterprises has a strong appeal to the populations of Central American neighbors where similar conditions prevail.[5]

8

"Stability," in short, means the security of "the upper classes and large foreign enterprises" in whose interests policy is designed. As guardian of order, the U.S. cannot tolerate such "instability," particularly when the infection shows signs of spreading, inspiring others to consider the needs of peasants and workers. As President Eisenhower and Secretary of State Dulles contemplated the danger to global security posed by Guatemala, they were given the first evidence of the spread of the virus: it was possible, they were informed, that "a strike situation" in Honduras might "have had inspiration and support from the Guatemalan side of the border."

Guatemala's aggression having thus been established, Washington had ample justification to impose a blockade to cleanse the hemisphere of this abomination. The blockade would not be in violation of international law, Attorney-General Herbert Brownell assured the President, because the "self-defense and self-preservation" of the United States were at risk under these grave circumstances. The blockade would therefore fall under article 51 of the UN Charter, which permits self-defense against armed attack until the Security Council has time to act against the threat to peace—by Guatemala. Such is the nature of international law, in the real world.

The basic problem, Gleijeses concludes in his scholarly study, was that Arbenz's "agrarian reform was proceeding well, the PGT [Communist Guatemala Workers Party to which Arbenz was close, though not a member] was gaining popular support, and basic freedoms were being upheld. It was an intolerable challenge to America's self-respect."[6] And, self-respect aside, these developments were in dramatic conflict with the explicit principles guiding policy, as already noted.

To be sure, the ritual reasons were trotted out to justify U.S. actions: the Soviet threat that served as a useful reflex from the Bolshevik takeover in 1917. The credibility of this appeal can readily be assessed by a look at what immediately preceded 1917, and what immediately followed the fall of the Berlin Wall in November 1989, eliminating any conceivable Soviet threat. In 1915-16, Woodrow Wilson, pursuing his commitment to self-determination, launched bloody and destructive Marine invasions of Haiti and the Dominican Republic in defense against "the Huns"—by accident, turning the two countries into U.S. plantations; earlier subversion and aggression was in defense against the British, the Chileans, the Spanish, and on back to the "merciless Indian savages" of the Declaration of Independence, in its most shameful passages. As the Soviet system disappeared from history, George Bush celebrated the fall of the Berlin Wall by invading Panama to restore the rule of a tiny European clique of bankers and narcotraffickers, who could be kept in power only "under the mantle of United States protection," as Washington recognized.[7] The Soviet threat having vanished beyond resurrection, Bush was courageously defending the United States against the arch-maniac Noriega. From 1917 to 1989 the "Soviet threat" was deployed to justify support for European fascism, a wide range of Third World monsters, and endless atrocities around the globe, on grounds so flimsy as to scarcely merit refutation.

The meaning of all of this can hardly escape a sane observer. But the natural conclusions, however transparent, are largely beyond the pale; within the bounds of the reigning Political Correctness, we may speak of "errors," "naiveté," "exaggerated fears," and the like, but nothing more. The record provides a remarkable example of how near-totalitarian effects can be achieved in a very free society.

It is indeed true that Communists were active during the Guatemalan democratic revolution of 1944-54, "almost certainly no more than 4,000, and perhaps substantially fewer," according to a 1955 U.S. intelligence summary (NIE, July 26, 1955). As Gleijeses noted, "basic freedoms were being upheld," including tolerance of a wide range of opinion. Such excessive liberalism has always been anathema to U.S. leaders, whose concept of democracy requires guarantees that there will be no challenge, however slight, to business control of the political system. A secret State Department intelligence report of 1955 explained the problem: the democratic leadership that had thankfully been overthrown had "insisted upon the maintenance of an open political system," thus allowing the communists to "expand their operations and appeal effectively to various sectors of the population." Neither the military "nor self-seeking politicians" were able to overcome this disorder of the body politic. Evidently, in the face of this threat, the global guardian of democracy could not refrain from intervention to restore "stability."

The Communists ("prominent journalists, congressmen, labor leaders, senior members" of the left political parties) were notable for "a combination of dynamism, intellect, and integrity that was and would remain unequalled in Guatemalan politics," Gleijeses writes, noting that these were precisely the conclusions of the U.S. embassy at the time as well as of journalists and scholars "whose anti-communist credentials are above suspicion." The Communist leaders "were very honest, very committed," a high U.S. embassy official commented: "This was the tragedy: the only people who were committed to hard work were those who were, by definition, our worst enemies." They were "our worst enemies" because they had entirely the wrong concept of who should be "the first beneficiaries of the development of a country's resources," as already discussed. Whether they were technically "communists" or not scarcely mattered. As Gleijeses aptly comments, "Just as the Indian was branded a savage beast to justify his exploitation, so those who sought social reform were branded communists to justify their persecution," a pattern so common throughout the world as scarcely to merit notice.[8]

The problem of demonstrating the threat of Communism was addressed forthrightly by U.S. embassy officer John Hill, who advised that the planned blockade would "enable us to stop ships including our own to such an extent that it will disrupt Guatemala's economy." That would lead either to a pro-U.S. coup or to increased Communist influence; the latter would in turn "justify...the U.S. to take strong measures," unilaterally if necessary.[9] We thus seek to destroy the Guatemalan economy so as to provoke either a coup restoring our control or some Communist reaction that will justify our violent response—in self-defense. This plan extends the earlier one: to keep Guatemala under constant threat, depriving it of any means of self-defense in the hope that it will appeal to the Russians for support as a last resort, in which case our blockade may unearth evidence of Russian shipment of arms to Guatemala, sure proof that it is about to conquer the hemisphere, entitling us to respond in self-defense.

The general technique has been adopted routinely, often with extreme clumsiness, but with little fear of exposure in a highly conformist political and intellectual culture, as the long record in Latin America and elsewhere demonstrates. Hill's proposal illustrates the fact that more intelligent elements are aware of the fraud used to beguile others and to defend oneself from unpleasant reality, though many are able to convince themselves of what it is convenient to believe, a talent that is useful for access to privilege and prestige.

Washington had for a time toyed with the possibility that Arbenz might be acceptable as President, despite his association with the much-despised democratic revolution that had been led by Juan José Arévalo, elected President in 1945. A 1949 analysis held that Arbenz was "essentially an opportunist" and "basically of an autocratic character." He had "no admixture of Indian blood" and "no real sympathy for the lower classes or for the many outside communists who have infiltrated Guatemala." Our kind of guy, in short. There was a chance that he might prove to "be a strong dictator...who could be truly ruthless if necessary" and would "rid Guatemala of its leftist penetration" and "remove from Guatemala some of the truly liberal gains of the revolution." His assumption of power "would probably mean the end of the coercion of U.S. capital, a return of Guatemala to cooperation with the United States, and the end of any personal freedom in Guatemala."

"The thrust of the argument was clear," Gleijeses comments: "Arbenz was an unsavory character with whom the United States could work well." But he soon "betrayed the hopes of the Truman administration," failing to be the "cynic" and "opportunist the Americans anticipated" and moving quickly to implement Latin America's first significant agrarian reform. "The more he accomplished, the closer he came to his destruction and the destruction of his dream."[10]

The destruction was consummated with the U.S.-run coup and aggression in June 1954. At home, "Republicans and Democrats sang the appropriate chorus in impressive bipartisan harmony," Gleijeses comments, while "the American press leaped into collective self-delusion and ardently embraced the lies of the State Department." The *New York Times*, fulfilling its role as the semi-official newspaper, was particularly servile and ridiculous, notably its leading thinker of the day, Arthur Krock. The reaction in Latin America and Europe was quite different, except for the dictatorships of Trujillo and Somoza; under the latter, even *La Prensa*, then an independent newspaper, shamelessly parroted the most vulgar U.S. propaganda.

For years, the *New York Times*, like its lesser colleagues, had been obediently following the line laid down by the State Department and the United Fruit Company (UFCO). Describing UFCO's success

14

in shaping U.S. perceptions, its chief Public Relations officer Thomas McCann commented that "it is difficult to make a convincing case for manipulation of the press when the victims proved so eager for the experience." Despite the miserable record, however, Eisenhower and Dulles were still not satisfied. They privately expressed their rage at the behavior of the *Times* and sought—successfully it appears—to have its correspondent Sydney Gruson removed for the period of the coup. The Soviet high command and top party officials were no less enraged by the lack of patriotism shown by the Soviet press during the invasion of Afghanistan.[11]

The consequences of the U.S. takeover were devastating. Some 8,000 peasants were murdered in two months in a terror campaign that targeted particularly UFCO union organizers and Indian village leaders. The U.S. embassy participated with great fervor, providing lists of "Communists" to be eliminated or imprisoned and tortured while Washington dedicated itself to making Guatemala "a showcase for democracy." The embassy was particularly outraged that 5 of the 11 members of the PGT Political Commission remained at large. "Of these eleven men, three are alive today," Gleijeses writes, the rest having been tortured and murdered, some dropped into the ocean from army transports after they were killed, which may have at least partially satisfied American blood lust. The Arbenz reforms were completely reversed and the democratic system shattered, never to recover, except in form. The nightmare returned, far more grim even than before.[12]

As these procedures were running their course, the *New York Times* praised the coup leader,

Castillo Armas, for his "sound decisions" and "progressive policies." The editors felt some qualms when Armas was elected president in October 1954 with 99.99% of the vote in a plebiscite run by the army. But, ever judicious, they cautioned against premature concern: "It is doubtless unfair to expect anything else so soon after a revolution against a Communist-dominated regime." The National Intelligence Estimate of July 26, 1955, on "probable developments in Guatemala" detected an impressive commitment of the military regime to "democratic forms and practices, to land reform, to the development of a modern economy, and to the protection of a free labor movement and other social gains." It simultaneously recognized that in the irrelevant real world, "the Guatemalan economy weakened considerably following the fall of Arbenz," the labor movement was "virtually destroyed" and "rural groups are having even more difficulty in obtaining favorable government action" with the destruction of peasant organizations and the denial of "the right to organize," democratic forms were being dismantled by violence and most of the population was disenfranchised, land reform was reversed, and the social gains of the democratic decade were abolished.

In such ways, the U.S. created a "showcase for democracy," with the chorus at home basking in the pride and self-adulation that is a standard concomitant of such exercises. The record is being replayed today, with even more enthusiasm, in glorification of the ghastly decade of U.S.-run atrocities that succeeded in demolishing a good part, though not all, of the democratic awakening of the 1970s, when the Central American rabble once again made the mis-

16

take of trying to take some control over their lives and fate.

Terror in Guatemala mounted again in the late 1960s, with active U.S. participation, leaving many thousands dead. The process resumed a decade later, soon reaching epic levels of barbarism as the U.S. campaign against democracy and social justice moved into high gear throughout the region. Over 440 villages were demolished, huge areas of the highlands were destroyed in a frenzy of possibly irreversible environmental devastation, and well over 100,000 civilians were killed or "disappeared," up to 150,000 according to the Church and others. All of this proceeded with the enthusiastic acclaim of the Reagan administration, who assured the public at the height of the horror that the most extreme murderers and torturers were "totally committed to democracy" and were receiving a "bum rap" from human rights organizations, the Church, and others who are soft on Communism. Assistant Secretary of State Thomas Enders, who has recently gained some notoriety after belated exposure of his role in covering up huge massacres in El Salvador, wrote that

> No one deny would the possibility [sic] of units of the military, in contravention of stated policy, having been involved in violations of human rights. What is important is that since March 23 [1982] the Government of Guatemala has committed itself to a new course and has made significant progress.

Enders's letter was distributed through the Guatemalan press, where, as Americas Watch pointed out in a bitterly critical reaction, it served to put at even greater risk the brave human rights

17

investigators who sought to survive the "significant progress" of the State Department's favorite killers. The press went along without few murmurs.[13]

There is no space to document adequately the "new course" that so entranced Mr. Enders. It was reviewed in October 1982 by Amnesty International, which reported that in widespread massacres, the new progressive regime had "destroyed entire villages, tortured and mutilated local people and carried out mass executions." For example, in one village troops "forced all the inhabitants into the courthouse, raped the women and beheaded the men, and then battered the children to death against rocks in a nearby river." Survivors of the Finca San Francisco massacre in July described how 300 people were killed, the women raped and shot or burned to death in houses put to the torch, the old people hacked to pieces with machetes, the children disemboweled. The last child, two or three years old, kept screaming after he was disemboweled so "the soldier grabbed a thick hard stick and bashed his head," then "smashed him against a tree trunk" so hard that his head "split open." The London *Economist* reported the "sadistic butchery" of Enders's "new course," meanwhile recommending that El Salvador "could copy" these methods with profit and that "liberal Americans" should at most call for "an easing of the political persecution of the centre—which played into the hands of the extreme left in the first place." The rest can perish in silence.

In a letter of July 27, Father Ronald Hennesy reviewed "a few of the happenings of just this month in just this parish," four months into the "new course" and just as Washington granted $11 million to the military regime to reward its "progress." He described how soldiers came to a village, took ten men, "tied their hands behind their back, cut their throats, and tossed them off the cliff." In another, "four tortured bodies were dumped on the road." In another, the army forced villagers to beat seven people to death with clubs, killing a 13-year-old boy for good measure. In another, "all of the men, with hands tied behind their backs, were escorted by the soldiers to one house, shot, stabbed, piled one on top of the other, and covered with burnable items of the very house, which were sprinkled with gasoline and set on fire. The women were treated the same as the men, stacked for burning. The other children were tied, one to another, and pulled alive into the flames of a third house by the soldiers."

And on, and on.

While Enders praised the "new course," his boss George Shultz looked on, displaying the steely integrity for which he is much admired. Or perhaps he was preparing his notes for his forthcoming trip to Panama to hail the election of his former student Nicolas Ardito Barletta as "initiating the process of democracy" after the election had been stolen by his (then-friend) Manuel Noriega with fraud and violence, saving the country from the actual victor, an "ultranationalist" Washington disliked.[14]

One of the grandest of the Guatemalan killers, General Héctor Gramajo, was granted a fellowship to Harvard's John F. Kennedy School of Government. There he gave an interview to the *Harvard International Review* in which he rejected criticisms of his role, which failed to recognize his contributions. He took personal credit for the "70%-

30% civil affairs program, used by the Guatemalan government during the 1980s to control people or organizations who disagreed with the government," outlining the doctrinal innovations he had introduced: "We have created a more humanitarian, less costly strategy, to be more compatible with the democratic system. We instituted civil affairs [in 1982] which provides development for 70% of the population, while we kill 30%. Before, the strategy was to kill 100%." This is a "more sophisticated means" than the previous crude assumption that you must "kill everyone to complete the job" of controlling dissent, he pointed out. Perhaps this new announced strategy is the "significant progress" that so impressed the State Department.

A "senior commander in the early 1980s, when the Guatemalan military was blamed for the deaths of tens of thousands of people, largely civilians," Gramajo "is seen as a moderate by the U.S. Embassy," Kenneth Freed reported in the *Los Angeles Times* in 1990, quoting a Western diplomat, and assuring us of Washington's "repugnance" at the actions of the security forces it supported and applauded. As a "moderate," Gramajo joins a distinguished company that includes Mussolini, Hitler, Suharto, and numerous other attractive folk who, it was thought, were serving U.S. interests. The *Washington Post* reports that many Guatemalan politicians expect Gramajo to win forthcoming elections, not unlikely if he is the State Department favorite, as widely rumored. Gramajo's image is also being prettified. He offered the *Post* a sanitized version of his interview on the 70%-30% program: "The effort of the government was to be 70% in development and 30% in the war effort. I was not referring to the people, just the effort." Before he had just expressed himself badly, before the Harvard grooming took effect.[15]

The goal of the massacres that peaked in the early 1980s was to prevent a recurrence of popular organization or any further thought of freedom or social reform. The Guatemalan military followed the model of the National Security States that had their roots in Kennedy administration policies: the recourse to state terror "to destroy permanently a perceived threat to the existing structure of socio-economic privilege by eliminating the political participation of the numerical majority..."[16] The toll since the U.S. regained control is commonly estimated at about 200,000 unarmed civilians killed or "disappeared." In the highlands, the record is unspeakable. In an amazing triumph of the human spirit, popular forces and leaders continue their struggle against U.S.-backed neo-Nazism.

Throughout, the task has been to put to rest, for once and for all, the heresies that had sprouted in Guatemala during the decade of democracy. They were reviewed by the National Intelligence Estimate of July 1955, already quoted, which found that "Most politically conscious Guatemalans believe that the US planned and underwrote the 1954 revolution," evidently not having read the State Department version as presented by the *New York Times*. More dangerous yet, "A keen sense of nationalism, at times verging on the irrational, colors Guatemalan politics... there is a strong tendency to attribute Guatemala's backwardness to foreign investors, especially those from the US. Even the most pro-US elements in the area are not immune to this type of extreme nationalism." No less serious was "the heritage of the revolution of 1944." "Many Guatemalans are passionately attached to the democratic-nationalist ideals of the 1944 revolution," particularly, to "the social and economic programs initiated by the Arévalo and Arbenz regimes." During these years of excessive democracy, "the social and economic needs of labor and the peasantry were articulated and exploited by the small Communist leadership" who "were able to promote measures which appeared to meet some of the aspirations of these groups," including "considerable progress in the organization of urban and rural unions" and "inducing the government to expropriate large tracts of land for distribution among the landless" in a successful agrarian reform.

Unfortunately, intelligence concludes, "there are probably not over 200,000 Guatemalans who are more than marginally politically conscious." Hence the prevalence of the strange delusions held by "many Guatemalans," including workers and peasants and even "most pro-US elements." And of the tiny minority who can comprehend the official U.S. version of reality and therefore qualify as at least "marginally politically conscious," "few understand the processes and responsibilities of democracy," so that "responsible democratic government is therefore difficult to achieve." The peons may still sink back to their puerile preference for democratically elected governments that promote measures to meet the aspirations of the overwhelming majority of the population.

Extreme as it was, the early phase of the terror

failed to get to the roots of the problem. A CIA analysis of 1965 deplored the "low level of intellectualism" in the country that makes the task of reeducation so difficult. As evidence, the Agency noted that "liberal groups...are overresponsive to 'Yankee imperialist' themes," perhaps because of "the long-term political and economic influence of US fruit companies in the country as well as by the US role in the Castillo Armas liberation"—the "liberation" by the CIA-run coup that overthrew the popular democratic government and reinstated the murderous rule of the military and oligarchy. The rot is persistent, and the leader of the Free World must dedicate itself to removing it forever.

As for the "showcase of democracy," an election was scheduled for 1963, but it was blocked by a military coup tolerated or backed by the Kennedy administration to prevent the participation of Juan José Arévalo, still suspect as soft on Communism though he had by then become an ardent admirer of the United States, now that it was led by "new men—men who studied at Harvard." An election did take place in 1966. Its effect was to extend military control over the country, setting off a huge wave of terror with direct U.S. participation. A 1985 election was proclaimed by the U.S. embassy to be the "final step in the reestablishment of democracy in Guatemala." The November 1990 elections ended in a draw between two right-wing candidates advocating the neo-liberal programs that the U.S. insists upon for the Third World. They managed to stir up 30% of the electorate (counting valid votes). In the runoff election won by Jorge Serrano, abstention was even higher.[17]

After Serrano's military-backed "self-coup" of May 1993 elicited fears of an aid cut-off, the Guatemalan military, who generally run the show behind a very thin screen, "opted to stay in the barracks" as popular forces impelled the Congress to elect Ramiro de León Carpio, Guatemala's human rights ombudsman, to complete Serrano's term. "Overarching credit for the peaceful transition," according to former *Times* Latin America correspondent Henry Raymont who was in Guatemala with the OAS mission, "goes to the civic movement" inspired by de León Carpio's "bold denunciations of human rights violations by the Serrano government," the "crucial ruling" by Supreme Electoral Tribunal president Arturo Herbruger declaring Serrano's acts unconstitutional, and "the daily protest marches led by labor leaders and Rigoberta Menchú." The Clinton administration "is taking excessive credit," he concludes, ignoring the courageous actions that led to "the triumph of the will of the people." "Guatemala was saved from this inept tyrant's apprentice by the courageous and decisive action of a handful of Guatemalans who, in the name of my country, I wish to thank," wrote the editor of the newsweekly *Cronica* that had been banned by Serrano.[18]

The army may have remained in the barracks, but "whether it will remain there remains to be seen," Raymont observes. De León Carpio's first act was to name as his new Defense Minister General Roberto Perussina, "a senior officer viewed by some diplomats and Guatemalan analysts as a leader of the harder-line faction within the army." U.S. aid, temporarily withheld, resumed. Perussina was replaced a few weeks later by an officer considered more moderate, though again with a dubious human rights record, a characteristic that few high officers lack. There are hopeful signs, but they will not materialize by themselves.[19]

The horrifying terror, which continues to the present, is only one aspect, one might even say a minor aspect, of the violence and abuse that we have imposed and maintained by force in this rich and potentially flourishing country. When we deplore the crimes of official enemies, such as the Khmer Rouge, we rightly count the numbers who died as a result of their brutal policies, not merely those killed outright, a minority of the victims. Similar calculations in Guatemala would yield an awesome figure. Merely to give a brief indication, Guatemala now boasts a higher level of child malnutrition than Haiti, according to UNICEF. The Health Ministry reports that 40% of students suffer from chronic malnutrition, while 2.5 million children in this country of 9 million suffer abuse that leads them to abandon school and become involved in crime, or live in the streets where they are subject to torture by security forces, reported to be "soaring."[20] A quarter of a million have been orphaned by political violence. 87% of the population live below the poverty line (up from 79% in 1980), 72% cannot afford a minimum diet (52% in 1980), 6 million have no access to health service, 3.6 million lack drinking water, and concentration of land ownership continues to rise (2% now control 70% of the land). Purchasing power in 1989 was 22% of its 1972 level, dropping still further as the neoliberal measures of the 1980s were intensified.

As terror improved the investment climate after the 1954 "liberation," U.S. advisers were able to impose the preferred "development model," with the right priorities. Export-oriented economic programs led to rapid growth in production of "nontraditional" agricultural commodities and beef for export, destruction of forests and subsistence agriculture, sharp increase in hunger and general misery, the world championship for DDT in mothers' milk (185 times World Health Organization limits), and gratifying balance sheets for U.S. agribusiness and local affiliates. Dr. Luís Genaro Morales, president of the Guatemalan Pediatric Association, adds that child trafficking "is becoming one of the principal nontraditional export products," generating $20 million of business a year. The International Human Rights Federation, after an inquiry in Guatemala, gave a more conservative estimate, reporting that about 300 children are kidnapped every year, taken to secret nurseries, then sold for adoption at about $10,000 per child. We may put aside here the macabre reports, common throughout much of Latin America from sources that are not easy to discount, about kidnapping of children for organ transplants.

Current economic plans, under the guidance of U.S. advisers, are intensifying this range of effects. We have much to be proud of in the "showplace of democracy" that we graciously instituted and maintained.

The reports of refugees and of the human rights activists who have somehow continued their work under atrocious conditions have provided a gruesome record of what has been happening in these terrible years. The shameful picture is extended in the personal testimonies of the compañeros and compañeras who, with awesome heroism that even their unassuming simplicity cannot disguise, turned to resistance against unending barbarism. As the picture comes to light, a sane person cannot fail to feel outrage and anger, despair that the human soul can harbor such depths of depravity. But other questions might come to the fore. Who created "the situation that gives rise to violence"? Who refused to listen to the screams of children being brutally murdered or dying from starvation and disease, because there are pleasanter things to do? Who paid taxes quietly and unthinkingly, helping to ensure that torture, massacre, and indescribable suffering continue, while doing nothing to end these crimes—or worse, justifying and abetting them? Who joined in the torrents of self-praise that pour forth in sickening abundance, keeping eyes carefully averted from what we have actually done with our huge resources and incomparable advantages? Who are the real barbarians?

Noam Chomsky
22 July 1993

Notes

1. For sources where not cited here, and much additional material, see my *Turning the Tide* (South End, 1985), *On Power and Ideology* (South End, 1986); *TheCulture of Terrorism* (South End, 1988); Necessary Illusions (South End, 1989); *Deterring Democracy* (Verso, 1991; Hill and Wang, extended paperback edition, 1992); *Year 501* (South End, 1993); Edward Herman and Noam Chomsky,

Manufacturing Consent (Pantheon, 1988). On Guatemala specifically, see Susanne Jonas, *The Battle for Guatemala* (Westview, 1991).

2. Piero Gleijeses, *Shattered Hope The Guatemalan Revolution and the United States, 1944-1954* (Princeton, 1991).

3. Gleijeses, *Politics and Culture in Guatemala* (Michigan, 1988), sponsored by the State Department.

4. NSC 5432, "U.S. Policy Toward Latin America," Aug. 18, 1954; its principles are reiterated elsewhere, often verbatim (e.g., NSC 5613/1, Sept. 25, 1956). See *On Power and Ideology* for more extensive discussion.

5. Gleijeses, *Shattered Hope,* 242, 365.

6. Ibid., 366.

7. Latin America specialist Steve Ropp, "Things Fall Apart: Panama after Noriega," *Current History,* March 1993.

8. *Politics and Culture.*

9. Bryce Wood, *The Dismantling of the Good Neighbor Policy* (Texas, 1985), 177.

10. Piero Gleijeses, *Shattered Hope*, 78f., 7, 125, 134.

11. Ibid., 367f. For illustrations of *Times* commentary, see *Turning the Tide,* 164f.; on the Gruson affair and administration charges, see *Necessary Illusions,* 322f.; on the Soviet counterpart, see *Manufacturing Consent,* 226f.

12. See particularly Jonas, *Battle.* Gleijeses, *Shattered Hope,* 388.

13. See Jonas, *op. cit.*; Enders, *Manufacturing Consent,* 77f.

14. *Turning the Tide,* chap. 1, sec. 4, for these and

28

numerous other examples; Hennesy, Jonathan Kwitny, *Endless Enemies* (Congdon & Weed, 1984), 235. Shultz, *Deterring Democracy*, 150-1.

15. *Year 501*, 29-30.

16. Lars Schoultz, *Human Rights and United States Policy toward Latin America* (Princeton, 1981), p. 7.

17. Arévalo, see Gleijeses, *Shattered Hope*, 394-5. Jonas, *op. cit.*

18. Tim Golden, *NYT*, May 26, June 7; Raymont, *Boston Globe*, June 14.

19. Tim Golden, *NYT*, June 8. See Guatemala Human Rights *Update*, #11/93, June 11; #11/1993, July 9, 1993 (Guatemala Human Rights Commission/USA).

20. Reuter, "Torture of Kids Reported Soaring in Guatemala," *Miami Herald*, Jan. 19, 1993; *Central America NewsPak*.

Author's Note

Who are the Guatemalan revolutionaries? What minds and hearts make up the organizations of the entity called the Unidad Revolucionaria Nacional Guatemalteca, the Guatemalan National Revolutionary Union (URNG)? What do they want? What do they think? How do they behave? Do people support them? Magazines, television, and newspapers in the United States reveal little about Guatemala and nothing about the *compañeros**
themselves. Not surprisingly, the various Latin American revolutions begin to blur together in the consciousness of the U.S. public. In the absence of concrete information, the image of a guerrilla emerges in foggy and stereotypical form, young and a bit macho, idealistic yet dogmatic, jaunty in a beret and dangerously armed.

In the early 1980s, I began to work with Guatemalan refugees who fled the terror of their country. To find supporting evidence for their political asylum applications, I traveled to Mexico gathering information and testimonies, visiting church organizations, and interviewing people at the refugee camps. Later, I moved to Guatemala itself. The human devastation that I witnessed is well documented in the annals of Amnesty International, in the regular reports of Americas Watch, and the denouncements of the Catholic Church. This book

*Compañero(a): Literally friend or companion. In Latin America, the term frequently refers to a person who shares one's ideals. The guerrillas use the term to refer to one another.

does not attempt to repeat the documentation. Rather, it attempts to tell a part of the story that, for many reasons, has always been concealed.

During my years in Guatemala, I came to know many people involved in the underground, in the revolution. They were men and women, old and young, professors and peasants, civil rights workers and Mayan villagers. Some are still living but many are now dead, either killed in combat or hunted down in the city streets. In the years since I was forced to leave the country, my contact with these revolutionaries has remained strong. I have come to know more and more of them, as individuals and as friends. To keep them safe from harm, the details of my connections and relationships with them can never be told—at least not until this terrible war has ended. But we know each other well and see each other with great frequency. For me, it has been a privilege.

This book is an anthology, a collection of oral histories. Throughout the years, there have been many difficult times, but also quiet times, opportunities to talk, swap stories, ask about each other's lives and dreams. I have written down those stories, just as they were told to me. For the sake of accuracy, I have included only accounts that were given to me first hand, and by people I had come to know personally. I have also included excerpts from the journal I kept during my time in Guatemala.

The stories are divided into four categories: Part I gives accounts about how and why people made the difficult and dangerous decision to work for their revolution; Part II describes earlier stages of the war, of conditions, hardships and battles in the early 1980s; Part III includes accounts and descriptions of present day life in the struggle, the changes made and the hopes for the future; Part IV discusses projects people can get involved with to change their plight. I have changed the names and places and other identifying details. I want this book to cause no deaths. Three of the stories are composites of several similar stories, blended together to avoid repetition. No other changes have been made. None of the people or the events is fictitious.

These are the stories of people I have come, through the years, to love and respect. So many gave their lives with only the hope that their sacrifices would lead to a new and better Guatemala. Some of those whose stories are in this book are now dead. They, and those who still survive, deserve to be known and remembered.

PART I
Heeding
the Call to Action

Note

The events described in the following stories took place, for the most part, during the late 1970s and early 1980s. The army unleashed its campaign of terror against all those seeking social change, whether armed revolutionaries or civilians attempting reforms through peaceful and legal means. Mayan civil rights workers died in the Spanish Embassy, cooperatives were destroyed, and rural health and literacy promoters disappeared, never to be seen again. Not even the Church was exempt: progressive priests were assassinated, and catechists were killed and abducted in terrifying numbers. Hardest hit of all were the Mayan villages of the highlands, which the army suspected of supporting the guerrilla movement. The village of San Francisco Nenton was wiped from the map in a single afternoon, leaving some three hundred men, women, and children dead amid the charred debris of the town hall. Hundreds of other villages disappeared as the army assaults against the civilian Mayan population reached geno- cidal proportions.

The citizens of Guatemala were faced with diffi- cult choices: submission, exile, or struggle. Given the mass destruction of all previous civilian reform efforts, many people chose the path of revolution, despite the personal risks involved. The following sto- ries illustrate how some reached this difficult deci- sion .

Anita

Come on now, don't be shy. I see you are looking at the scars on my face. A big bullet blew off half
my jaw about five years ago during an army
ambush. As a doctor, I can tell you it was hell to
repair all the damage—more than a dozen full-anes-
thesia surgeries in a Costa Rican hospital. I had
family there, so I was lucky. Even though they
didn't approve, they provided me with papers and a
cover story for the injury. It took years, though. All I
really remember from that period is rolling in and
out of surgery, and lifting weights and working out
in between operations to keep up my strength.

Here, sit down and drink some of this coffee
and I'll tell you the whole story. This is good
Guatemalan coffee, hard to get here, so I hope you
enjoy it. Try this fruit too, from our garden. There's
nothing wrong with my jaw now, so we can talk all
afternoon, if you like.

My childhood was a little rough and tumble. I
never really knew my father. He had abandoned my
mother and all of us children, and only came to the
house from time to time when he was drunk, to
abuse her and take her hard earned money. She
never complained much, because she assumed that
men were just that way. And besides, she was
strong enough to handle anything. She was a tough,
beautiful peasant woman who could manage a
twenty-hour work day and five small children without even slowing down. And she was smart, too.
Even with the meager education she had, she started her own successful business and kept it going.

35

Years later, it was she who saved my life, no questions asked, and got me out of the country to safety. And it was she, no questions asked, who reconnected me to the underground once I was strong enough to go back to war. I know that it is from her example that I developed my opinions on feminism and the role of women.

I joined the underground during my last year of medical school. I had just finished a rotation up in the jungle areas with the peasant cooperatives, and had learned a lot. What an eye opener that year was! It had been very difficult. My school supervisor hated women medical students and had sent me to the most remote regions in hopes that I would give up. Instead, though, I thrived, and came to love the villagers who took me in and cared for me. I loved their gentle ways, and their generosity, and I saw the unfairness and repression that they suffered. I never forgot it, even after I returned to the capital for my last year of study. And with my new awareness, I saw the things in the city that, perhaps, I hadn't wanted to see before.

I lived not far from a small union office, and on the way to the hospital each morning, I saw the fresh black ribbons on the union door, the new photographs, signaling yet another member dragged off to an ugly death in the middle of the night. And I saw the morgues. The tortures that had been inflicted on those poor people, the expressions on those dead faces, I will never forget. It is because of the morgues, I am positive, that so many of us medical students, and yes, even professors, joined up with the underground that year. Look, here is my graduation photo. See the two men handing me my diploma? They are both dead now; they were part of the city underground, but I didn't know it then. The two students next to me? They were with the guerrillas, too. I think they went to the mountains. None of us knew about each other, for security reasons. But I know now, and when I look at this photo, I feel doubly proud. Proud of the diploma and my completed studies, proud of all of us in the group, and proud of the courage represented in this image. It makes me happy to show it to you. I want these people remembered.

At first I worked in the city, with another medical student named Melissa. We had many small tasks: treating a wounded person brought in from the mountains, hiding medicines and passing them on, working in the clandestine clinics. It was all very dangerous. To be caught with medicines outside of the hospital meant death by torture. To be found treating a wounded combatant meant an immediate bullet. We both understood this, but we gave each other so much support, so much love. We were more than sisters. I still weep when I think of Melissa.

I don't know how she was found out, but she was. Things had grown so terrible in the city. Every day, our people were captured and tortured. And under that kind of torture, if people do not die quickly, they will talk. They cannot help it. So perhaps someone spoke of her, described her, gave away her next meeting point. Who knows—it doesn't matter. I found her in the morgue with so many others. She was naked and battered, her face bluish from strangulation, small razor cuts and cigarette burns up and down her arms and legs. Her autopsy report showed vaginal slashes, as if her captors, once finished with her themselves, had raped her with a broken bottle. Her eyes were gone, the sockets filled with mud. Looking down at her, I felt all my physician's arts were useless. It is so strange—it was not her injuries that hurt me the most. She was the same as all the others, there on the metal slabs that day. I had grown used to it. The pain was just from the loss of her, the loss for all of us left living.

That was the day I left for the mountains. I knew they would be coming for me soon. But that wasn't the real reason I left. I knew I could die just as quickly in the mountains. I could have fled the country to safety, but I chose not to. I had made a decision—I had decided to fight. I had decided that when those animals came looking for me, to kill me in that way, by God they were going to find me with a gun in my hands.

The Old Man

Well, yes, certainly I have a favorite story. It's about tall tales, and I'll be glad to tell it to you. I just want to make it clear that this story is not a tall tale itself, just a story about tall tales, or rather, about tales I thought were tall tales, but which turned out to be completely true. You'll probably be thinking the same thing when you hear this, so that's why I'm telling you ahead of time that this really happened.

Well anyway, this started many years ago, in the city. It was back in the early 1980s when things were really, really bad for us. I was in the underground. My older brother had brought me in. I had joined because I would do anything he asked me to do, and because I knew as well as anybody else that things in Guatemala had to change. I had been with the student activists on campus for awhile, until they started being gunned down in the streets, and I had to quit, to cool off. That's when my brother came and talked with me about a real revolution, and I knew he was right. He was killed the next week, but I won't tell you about that. That is not my favorite story.

So anyway, I was young and angry, and I really threw myself into my work with the movement. I was doing very good work, but doing it very maniacally, without balance. This worried my *responsable*, and so one day, as recognition for my efforts and also to give me perspective, he took me to see a very special old man, one of the founders of the movement.

This really was a pretty amazing old man. When I first saw him, I couldn't believe my eyes. He was just a frail old guy dressed in loose work pants and gardening slippers, kneeling over a flower bed with his scruffy old dog at his side. When he stood up, though, he was very straight, with very steady dark eyes over his loose, old man's lips. He walked right up to me and embraced me and led me into the kitchen of his house as if he had known me for many years.

Inside, he made me a big pot of Guatemalan coffee and fed me, and asked me some questions about my work and my life. Then he sat back and started telling me stories, one after the other, some hilarious, some hair-raising, all of them incredible, about his life in the movement. These stories were just too wild, but the old man was so engaging, such a great story-teller, that I couldn't help sitting back, too, relaxing, laughing, and enjoying myself. I was having a really wonderful time, but I knew there was no way, absolutely no way, that all of these stories could be true. Somehow that made me enjoy myself all the more. It was like going to the movies with my grandfather, only the stories were also very inspiring, even though they made me laugh.

I don't remember all of the stories now, but there was one about his carrying a secret military message, very urgent, hidden in a bottle of mayonnaise in a big picnic basket. He ran into an army checkpoint, very bad luck, but almost got through it because he was old and harmless looking. Almost but not quite. At the last minute they grabbed him, and when they didn't like his answers they started torturing him. He insisted on his story though, that he was going to visit a relative with military connections, and finally, they let him go. As if this wasn't enough, he demanded his food back, and kept whining about it until finally the lieutenant yelled "here's your damned food!" and started throwing the stuff at him—the bread, the cheese, the fruit, and yes, the mayonnaise bottle. "Hah!" said the old man "Thank God the bottle didn't break".

"Hah," I thought to myself, "This old man tells the wildest stories I've ever heard." But I loved every minute of it. And by the end of the afternoon, I realized this man had done something really amazing with all his stories. He had pulled me in, opened my eyes, woven me into this incredible web of experiences that all of us in the movement share. All of a sudden I was not alone with my pain and my fear.

Well, finally it was growing late, and I had to leave. The old man followed me out the door and we embraced warmly. I didn't ask if I would ever see him again. As I walked away towards the corner where I was to wait for my ride, he returned to his flowerbed with his trusty mutt. It was then that I heard the sirens, and saw the army trucks come flying up the street towards us. The trucks were full of screaming soldiers, guns at the ready, and I knew they had come for us. I also knew not to run, so I just kept walking towards the corner, and miraculously, they roared past me without so much as a sidewards glance. Then my heart really sank, because I knew they must be coming for the old man. And sure enough, they pulled to a screeching stop on his front lawn. He was still kneeling over the flowerbed when the soldiers began leaping out of the truck.

The neighborhood had gone deadly quiet. I knew I should keep walking and not look back, but I ducked behind a wall and tried to at least see the license plate numbers on the trucks. As if this would make any difference! I was weeping, positive that I was going to see this wonderful human being beaten half to death and then dragged off to die in some secret prison, just like my brother had died. It was unbearable. As I watched, though, the old man rose gently to his feet and faced the group of soldiers racing up the lawn towards him. Most of them ran right past him, straight into the house, but a group of about eight shoved their rifles into his face. The lieutenant was wild-eyed. "Get the fuck out of here old man—things are going to get ugly!" he shrieked. The old man didn't bat an eye. "Sí, *Comandante*, sí." That was all he said. Then he just picked up his little dog and shuffled off down the street without ever even looking back. The rest of the soldiers ran into the house then too, and I could hear them smashing furniture and cursing as I ran off. I guess they were expecting someone who looked more like Che.

It was many years before I would see the old man again. Not long after that things became impossible for me in the city and I had to leave for the mountains. But I saw him once, in a house for the wounded, strengthening the young combatants with his stories and his vision, just as he did for me. You should hear him tell the story about that day. He has everyone spellbound, of course. "*Ocho carabinas! Ocho!*" He tells them all, waving eight fingers in the air. "And they still told me to get lost!" And naturally everyone bursts out laughing, because it really is very funny, even though it didn't seem too funny at the time. And I imagine that a lot of the young ones wonder if this isn't just a tall tale. But I know better now. I realize all those stories he told me that day were true to the last word. I also know it doesn't really matter. Because the gift we all receive from this incredible, brave old man is his vision, and perhaps, most importantly, the ability to see ourselves and our experiences with a sense of humor.

Lara

I saw my brother off to the capital a few days before he was killed there. The army burned him to death, him and the other villagers who had gone on the march with him. I remember he was wearing the clothes I had scrubbed for him the day before and he was carrying a sack filled with the food I had prepared, big corn tortillas with black beans inside. I had made his favorite foods because he was special to me. I was still very young then, more girl than woman, and I didn't know that the food and the clean clothes would be my last gift of love to him.

Why was he special to me? Because he taught me to read and write. He told me that women, too, should use their lives productively, to serve our people, to work for a better future for our children. He told me that our people are not stupid, and our language is not backwards, that we are the descendants of the Maya, who had a great civilization. He taught me to think for myself. He was a member of the CUC, or the Campesino Unity Committee, an organization they had formed to work for better conditions for us up in the highlands. Sometimes I went to the meetings with him, but really only to listen and to be with him. It was all very exciting, but confusing, too. I was still too young to take any real steps towards activism myself.

My brother and the others left our village that day because there had been killings by the death squads in our area. They went, unarmed, to the capital to protest the repression of our people, to speak up for our needs. They went into the Spanish

Embassy, to occupy the building and talk with the politicians and the press. Even though it was peaceful, the security forces stormed the building and a fire broke out. They would not put out the fire. All of our people died in there, burned to death. My brother burned with the others.

I came to the capital to find him as soon as I heard. When I arrived, I found them all laid out in a row, all those burned bodies. It was hard to know which body was his, but I knew from the shoes and, well, I just knew. He was all charred and so very small, but I knew him. A journalist held me close and told me not to cry, but all I could think of was how could I not cry, with my brother laying there like that, all burned to nothingness? What does this journalist know about my brother and our people, telling me not to cry?

When I went back to our village, it was not the same for me. I remembered all of my brother's words about serving our people, but I thought that the CUC was not the answer. I tried the church for a while, working with my cousin. She was preaching about the rights of the poor. Then, when she, too, came under threats from the army, I knew what to do. I had been thinking so much and with so much confusion, but I had no confusion anymore. I left my clothing behind, the skirt and *huipil* I had woven myself, and put on pants and a man's shirt. I cut my long hair and picked up a rifle, and I went to the mountains to fight. I was very young, but the *compañeros* accepted me because my thinking was so clear.

I fought in the mountains for many years. I could tell you so many stories about people much better and more important than I am, much more deserving for you to write about them. If you come back, I will tell you these stories. But for today I ask only this. I am here in this city because I was in poor health. The *compañeros* brought me down here to recover, but it was during a very bad period, and the people I was staying with were killed. I have been in hiding ever since—more than two years now. For me it is very dangerous to make inquiries. But I am in good health and it is time for me to return to the mountains. The war is not over yet, and our revolution is real, not just a child's dream. It is as real as all of us that you see; we are poor but we are real. You are a writer, you know others. You are safe because you are a foreigner. Take this tape and these names—my false names, and the names of the people I was with, and pass them on to the others. Here is a map. They can find me there and follow me to a safer place where we can talk. Send these messages for me. You will not be sorry, and there is still much work for me to do.

Manuel

Yes, it's true that I was a priest before I joined the underground. I was a priest for many years, in fact. You laugh, but I am not the only one here with a surprising background. You will see, as you talk to more and more of us, how many of us were in the civil, popular movements first. But I don't blame you for smiling. I have to laugh myself when I remember the crazy twists and turns my life took for a while. One likes to think that everything evolves in order, with rational decisions. But of course, things rarely turn out that way.

As I said, I was a priest for many years. In fact, I was raised to be a priest—I was educated in a very traditional seminary. It was a strict upbringing, but I do not complain. It was deeply rooted in the concepts of love and service to mankind, values that guide my thoughts and choices to this day. It was a good beginning, although of course, there was so much left to learn later on. It was as a priest, a very young and idealistic priest, that I first moved out to the jungles to work with the people. And of course it was the people who ended up educating and working with me.

I had decided in the beginning to start a small literacy project to teach the people to read and write. Since they all spoke one of the Mayan languages, I first had to study and learn some of their languages myself so that I could communicate with them. I met with some of the village leaders to discuss the idea of the project and they were in favor of it. For nearly a year I prepared myself, studying and learning about how to teach literacy, meeting with the elders. And then I moved up there, into the jungle region, into one of their villages. And you would not believe how they received me, with such gentleness and patience. They built me a house, taught me to survive, and showed me their ways as they came to trust me. With them there was no racism, no antagonism toward outsiders. They just waited quietly, watching me, to see how I would turn out. And meanwhile they gave me a home. And such love!

You would not believe how the first project went. They knew that I was coming to teach reading and writing, and when I arrived the village had already organized itself. Ten members of the community had been selected to learn first and were excused from community work for the time they were to study. The others carried their work load for them. In return, they studied. I mean they really studied. After ten days they could read and write. Not well, not quickly, but they could read and write. I was dumbfounded. And the villagers had already arranged for how these ten were now to teach another group of ten each, and so on, until the community was educated. I had come with so many ideas about community organizing, community spirit, but these people were far ahead of me. I had not known these things about the Mayans—the way they think and act as one united people, the way they stick together and care for each other, the remarkable level of commitment they have for one another. And as time passed my paternalism had to crumble. I fell wildly in love with these villagers, with their kindly, gentle ways. And so the years went by.

I would never have left if the army had not arrived. I would have stayed forever as a jungle priest, happy with my work and my life. But there was trouble over the land. The villagers had been there for generations, sweating and laboring to change the land from the malarial swamp it was, into decent, farmable lands. They had built up their village, organized some medical care, and communally purchased equipment and machinery. It was working. Out of nothing they had created a decent life, poor but decent.

And now the wealthy families nearby began to claim that the land was theirs, and the army came to support those claims. People began to be threatened. Some were killed, some houses burned. On a particularly bad night, I told the elders that we should start burning the houses of the rich, to see how they liked that kind of treatment. Hah! I was such a young hothead, even if I was a priest. Fortunately, the elders were older and wiser. They nodded gravely at my suggestion, and went on to discuss other matters, and of course we never burned down anything at all. This was not their way. So we tried legal channels instead, but the people were cheated. The courts mistranslated their documents to state that they were relinquishing their lands instead of claiming them as their own. I began to travel to the capital to rouse support from old colleagues, people in the government now, people at the university. I was in a righteous rage, sure of myself, determined to save this community I had come to so love. I thought nothing could stop me.

But the repression grew worse. Throughout our

whole region there was death and destruction. I was working wildly, near despair. It was then that I received word that the army had decided to kill me. I would not be the first priest to die in Guatemala—several others, even foreigners, had already died here, assassinated. A woman came to tell me, the wife of a soldier involved in the plans. She had heard them plotting in her back room, and being a religious woman, had come to warn me. And so suddenly, it was time to leave. I was not even surprised, for it had been a long time that things had been leading to this. But to leave, to leave these people behind after all these years, after all we had been through! They were my family, my friends, my teachers. It was like cutting off my own arms. But in the end it was they themselves who convinced me to leave. I could help them no more, I could only die here. And this I knew was the truth.

And so I left, fleeing underground to the capital to the homes of some old friends. I had heard of a new resistance movement starting up, one that focused heavily on recognition of Indian rights and that was composed mostly of Mayan villagers just like the ones I had left. I asked my friends about this, demanding information, determined to find these people. They laughed gently at me, embracing me and shaking their heads. "Manuel," they told me, "Those people you are looking for are back there, right back up there where you have been all these years."

I was very surprised, of course, but I returned with the underground back to my own area, and sure enough, found the people I was looking for. It was a new world, disorienting in many ways. But it was the same people, the same gentleness, the same kindly and affectionate ways I had always loved in them. And just as they had done so many years before, when I thought to save the world with my literacy project, they reached out to me and pulled me into a new life.

And so now, fifteen years later, I am still with the guerrillas, still with the people I have always loved. They are no longer tilling their lands, and I am no longer saying Mass, but we are still together, struggling for our community, struggling for a better future for our people. In the end, my life is different and yet unchanged—I still love, and I still serve.

Sara

What am I studying here? Well, the history of our people, current events, the political situation in our region. Our materials, too—I mean the literature of our organization. Yesterday we studied the materials on racism, for example, and had a long talk about this. We saw the pyramids last week. I like drawing and painting. And I have been learning some radio science, too. I learned to read and write in the mountains and to speak Spanish. The *compas* there taught me when I first arrived. I learned two other languages there, also. I am twenty-two years old now. I came down to study for a while because I had been in the mountains since I turned sixteen. Well yes, of course I want to go back. The mountains are my home, and the *compas* there are my family. That's why I didn't want to come down earlier. But we must all take the time to learn new things, to do some thinking, to become more productive. I am glad to be here.

Why did I leave home so young? Well, I will tell you about it. I was from a very small village, a Mayan village. I grew up speaking our people's language, and wearing the *huipil* and *falda* I had woven myself, with the colors and symbols of our town. My mother had taught me to weave and taught me the meaning of each ancient symbol, just as her mother had taught her. My older brother taught me about the wild plants and herbs, which ones to eat for food when the crops failed, which ones to use for sickness. We worked the fields—all of us—my brothers and sisters, my elderly father, all of the other villagers, too. It was a hard life with much labor and no medicines or public services. Outside the village, the *ladinos* mocked us for being *indios*, dirty and stupid. And there was always hunger. But we were a close-knit community. We took care of each other.

But then the army came, and with them, so much repression. I was not twelve yet, and did not understand everything very well. But I saw the bodies of our neighbors hanging in the trees at dawn. Just hanging there, dead, for us to see all the blood, all the terrible wounds. I saw. We all saw, and we were very afraid, very sad, and underneath it all very angry. How could the army do these things to our people! But what could we do? We had no way to defend ourselves, no guns, no rights. And when my older brothers came to me one night to say they had to leave, even though I didn't understand everything they said to me, I knew they were right. They told me they were going away to the mountains, to fight the army. They told me they were going to fight for a new life for all of our people, so that there could be schools, doctors for when we grew sick, fair treatment for all of us. And no more killings, no more burning houses. And so even though I was too young to understand these things very well, and I was crying to see them leave us, I knew they were right. I wanted them to go and fight for us.

Things grew worse and worse for our village. The army kept coming back, over and over again, to kill and beat and burn. They said we were all subversives, even the children. And after a while, we didn't dare sleep in our homes at night. It wasn't safe anymore. So we would work in the fields, sneak home for some food, then we would slip away to sleep far from the village, hidden in the tall corn plants. Only our father would stay behind, because he was so old and sick he could barely walk. He didn't want to slow us down, and he wouldn't let us carry him. So we would lie there at night, and when we heard screams or saw the smoke from a burning house, we could only hope he was surviving the night.

It was then that I began to dream. Like I said, I was too young to understand everything my brothers had told me, but I began to dream these incredible dreams anyway, about what I imagined a revolution would be like. The dreams were so beautiful, so full of color, and happiness and hope. I would wake up so full of hope from these dreams. And it was in this way that I decided that I, too, must go to the mountains and fight with my brothers. The first time I left to find the guerrillas, I was twelve years old. Naturally, they sent me home. But the same dreams stayed with me, and I never changed my ideas. I waited for three years. And then, when I found a way to connect with another group in the underground, I ran away again. And this time, I convinced them to let me stay. I was just short of sixteen, and lied about my age. The *compas* were all very kind to me in the mountains. But of course, I really was too young.

I had never imagined how hard it would be, how cold at night, how heavy the packs. No one spoke my dialect of Mayan, so at first it was hard to comfort me. And I missed my family and the other villagers so terribly. I cried and cried. And all they could do was hold me and comfort me as best they could. And then I began to learn. I learned Spanish so I could speak with the others. I listened to the discussions, learned to read books. I grew stronger and got used to the cold. And the *compas* helped me through all of the hard times. They helped me to carry, to learn to set my tent straight, to go unafraid into combat with them. And so these *compas* became my new family, my new village.

All the same, they could not get me to leave my traditional skirt and colored *huipil* behind. They were all I had left of the old life, and I hung onto them no matter what anybody said to me. I insisted that I could march and climb the mountains in that straight, long skirt. I paid no attention when they told me what a good target for bullets I was, all dressed in red and purple like that. I was a stubborn as a burro. So finally, to save me from myself, Abigail, the woman sharing my tent, had to trick me. It was easy to do, because I trusted her completely. She was like my own sister to me. Well, she took me bathing and we left our clothing on the riverbank while two other women stood guard. Then she distracted me with funny stories until the others could take my clothes and hide them. When I came out of the water, there was a new uniform, olive green and neatly folded, waiting for me. I cried, but she held me close, and explained that my clothes were buried in a very safe place that only she knew about, and that when the war ended, she would go and fetch them for me. And because Abigail was my sister, and because she always kept her word, and because of course, no one can mountain climb very well in a long skirt, I was satisfied. Abigail is long dead now—she died in combat. So she cannot keep her word and fetch my clothes. But

I will always love her, for the way she helped me through the hard times, for the way she loved me.

When I turned sixteen, the *compas* gave me a special celebration. They gave me extra food they had brought from the villages they had traveled through. A packet of cookies and some dried fruits. They embraced me and told me how glad they were that I was with them, and how they respected me and valued me for making it through the hard times. And then they gave me a surprise. One of the *compas*, David, had been to his home village to connect with other *compas*, and his brother had sent back a doll for me. It was a small cloth doll, brand new, with long braids and a bright skirt. It was the first doll I ever had. I was so moved, so pleased. I tied her to my backpack and would not be parted from her. It was not so much to play with her that I loved her. It was the feelings of the *compas* that I could sense every time I looked at her. So for many years, I carried her on one side of my pack, with my rifle slung across the other. And no matter how much the other *compas* teased me about her, I never took her down.

Jorge

My first language is Canjobal. From up here in the mountains, I can say that with pride. Certainly my family raised me to speak it with pride. But the teachers in the schools, down in the cities, and the other, wealthier, *ladino* students, for them it was a reason to punish me, to humiliate me. It was Spanish, or Castellano if you please, and if my cousin and I were caught murmuring to each other in our own tongue, we were either jeered or beaten. To them, we were never Mayan, only *indios*, no matter how we succeeded at our studies. Fortunately, we came from strong families, and they never let us forget who we really were.

Both Mariella and I had grown up in the same village, in the highlands. The land there is very green, very beautiful, and good for the growing of many things. But even so, we were all very poor. It takes cash to buy fertilizers and equipment. Cash to bring the crops to the market from a far-away highland village. Any profits we might make were lost to the middlemen in the cities. I remember hearing the elders talking, even when I was a small child, about the need to organize ourselves, to pool monies, to buy a village generator and a village truck to haul our own crops with. After all, we shared everything else. We worked community fields together, built our homes together, made community decisions all together. It was our way of doing things. To this day, I think of these ways as a model for our future, for a new society where we can all respect each other, where we can all care for each other, instead of struggling like beasts to enrich ourselves at the cost of another human's suffering.

Perhaps my father had the same dreams, because very early on, he sent Mariella and me away to a church-run school in the city. We had just finished the fourth grade, both of us with very good notes, and the priest had gone to speak with my father about giving us a scholarship. Mariella's father had died of fever many years before, and her family was living with mine. My father made the decision for us both. We were to leave the village and study very hard, so that one day we could return and help our people to have a better life. We, of course, did not want to go at all. To leave our village was unthinkable. And it was a very unusual decision, really. Three or four years of school was more than either of my parents had, and it was a lot for most of our people. We all went to school when we could, but we had to work the fields to survive, so work always came first. To send both of us away would mean hard times for our family. They would have to carry their own work loads as well as ours, and my mother was already ill. But my father was determined. For our lives to get better, we must sacrifice, he explained. The family would sacrifice by working still harder, we were to sacrifice by studying very seriously, and learning things that would help our village. And so the community gave us a going away party, with good food and music from the *marimba*. My mother sewed us each one set of new clothes. And then we found ourselves on a rickety bus careening down the green mountainsides to the city. The trip took fourteen hours, and all the way we wept.

Heeding the Call to Action

Our school years were good in many ways. The teachers were strict, but they taught us many things. We learned about city life, about telephones and trains and banks. We listened to what the people on the streets were saying, and learned politics and current events. We learned about the rest of our own country, our natural resources, our history. We read and read. But we were never really accepted. Even the friendliest of the *ladinos* saw us as clay—clay for assimilation into their own culture. So there was a constant, and silent, tug of war. I reacted by retreating into my studies. Mariella fought. She was in the girls' wing, but we met every evening to whisper confidences and remember our home. Our family came to see us when they could, and we would talk until the early hours. They would teach us what we would have learned if we were still in our village—medicinal herbs, wild plants, our ancestral history.

We did well at school, but even when we finished secondary school my father would not let us return home. He packed us off to the university in the capital to learn more. He was older now, and very tired, but still, he would not let us come home to take care of him. The neighbors were helping, he told us, because they knew we would be coming back soon and would help them with all our new learning. We were to go to the university, and so we did. Mariella studied to become a social worker and I studied agronomy. We worked during the days and studied and took our classes at night. Mariella became very beautiful, but apart from that, all those years in the city did not change us at all.

And then, suddenly, we were finished and my

father and our neighbors were embracing us and welcoming us back, offering us special foods and presenting us with the woven clothing of our village. My mother had died the year before, her lungs destroyed by years of tuberculosis, no money, and no medicine. So the neighbors had woven the cloth in her place, to welcome us back to our village.

We went straight to work, especially Mariella. Always the stronger of the two of us, she plunged into her organizing work with the incredible energies she had stored up over the years. She set to work organizing a village co-op to buy better seeds and fertilizers. She got us money from a foreign foundation and bought the co-op a truck to carry the crops to market. The commercial truckers grew angry with her for that but she didn't care. Then she set to work to negotiate for better prices from the business people in the cities and got other, nearby villages to work with her. No one would sell until everyone got a fair price. The co-op saved and saved until there was money to buy harvesting equipment we had to rent before. I worked with her night and day, and the villagers were very happy. But of course, the businessmen and the big companies were not happy with us at all. They were especially not happy with Mariella, or with the co-op. They said the co-op was a communist organization, and that Mariella and I were subversives.

Then the threats began. One night the truck was burned. Later, a villager was found decapitated on the road to the city. But Mariella wouldn't quit, wouldn't even slow down. To her, the time for change had come, and just as our village had sacrificed for us, she was going to fight for them. She reported the killing to the church in the city. She began to meet with Indian cooperatives from other areas and became involved in the movement for racial equality for our people. After all, she said, we are 60 percent of the population here, and we do all of the work. Once she came back from the city and told me what she had heard of the underground resistance movement. The guerrillas were getting stronger, she told me. They are fighting for us. Their soldiers are all our own people. We marveled at this for a very long time, and wished we could meet them, but had no idea how. In Guatemala, it is a very dangerous thing to try to find out about the guerrillas.

Then one day, Mariella came to me, thrilled. A young man had come to the village to find her. He said he had been sent by someone in the other co-op she had visited the month before. He knew the right names, the right code words for safety and for trust. He told her he was a guerrilla, sent down from the mountains to talk to the people. He wanted to tell the villagers what the movement was about, what they were fighting for. Was there a popular organization there? Yes, she told him, the village cooperative. How many leaders in the co-op? About twenty, she answered. Would they be interested in listening to him? Yes, she was certain they would want to learn about this new movement. Good. Tomorrow at two, at the town hall? Yes, that would be fine.

I was afraid, but did not know why. We did not know this young man. Why had he come to us? Things with the army were becoming so difficult. They would kill us if they found out about this meeting. We did not know anyone in the guerrilla movement, so how could we tell if this man was truly a member or not? We had no way to judge him. Mariella listened carefully, and we talked late into the night. But in the end she decided to go. He knew the codes. It was only a meeting, after all, she reasoned. No one was doing anything but listening to what the man had to say. And we needed to know about this movement. She was convinced that the underground would become an important force in our country, and wanted to learn more about it. It was dangerous, but everything was dangerous in these days. We must have courage. And so she convinced me.

The next day I was in my small green house when I heard the screams and shouts begin. A young girl, bleeding from a blow to the mouth ran up the hill to me, sobbing. The army had come with the stranger. It was, after all, a trick. They were rounding up all of the co-op members and loading them into a truck. I must hide—they were looking for me. I ran into the tall corn plants and up a slope where I could see what was happening in the center of the village. The co-op building that we had all built together was burning. The army vehicle was there, the back opened up like a cattle truck. The soldiers were screaming obscenities and dragging the people inside. The other villagers were begging and pleading for their relatives. An old woman hung onto her son and was clubbed to the ground. My uncle reached out for his daughter, and a soldier slashed his face with a bayonet. None of our people had guns, only their voices to plead for mercy, to beg for the lives of their family. I saw Mariella then, bending over the old man. The soldiers fell on her, dragging her to the truck. It took three of them to drag her, she fought so hard. She looked once towards where I was hiding. Could she have known I was there? Her beautiful face was covered with blood from a blow to her head. I started up to run to her, but the village girl next to me pulled me down and held my face against her shoulder, so I couldn't see anything else. Two other villagers who had hidden with us held my arms. When I looked up again the truck was gone, with nineteen of our people.

We went to the church. They tried to help us but could do nothing. I went to the army, desperate, but they denied that they had any of our villagers. Mariella must have run off with some sweetheart without telling me, they said. I tried at some government offices, but we were under a military government, and they told me the same thing. When I kept asking, they threatened me, and I knew they meant it. There was no place else to go, no human rights groups in Guatemala, no Red Cross, no nothing. Finally our village received word that a group of bodies had been found far away, on the coast, the sea birds picking at them. I started to go, then realized that if Mariella was there I didn't want to know it. In my mind at least, she was still alive.

Our village never recovered. It was as if our communal heart had been cut out. We could have rebuilt the co-op, but the soldiers kept coming back and telling us it was subversive. I tried to keep working, but for what? We needed so much more than new strains of corn. I began remembering all the stories my father used to tell us when he visited in the city, about how our ancestors had fought against the conquistadors for the last five hundred years, how Guatemala is one of the few places where our people have survived, how we survived because we never stopped struggling against the invaders. And so I began to wait for the real guerrillas to reach our village. And when they finally did, I knew I could trust them. They were villagers like us, the same eyes, the same hair. They spoke our language. They wanted the same things we wanted. The same things Mariella had always wanted. And so when they packed up to leave, I asked them for a rifle and followed them out of the village.

I have been up here for more than ten years now. Up here, all languages are spoken, all cultures are respected. Mayan and *ladino*, we are together here, all dreaming of the same new world, where our children can live differently. So much has happened, I could talk for hours and hours. Will I ever come down? Only after the triumph. Only after the army is driven from our lands and we can start over again. So many of us were killed in the early days. Mariella, the *compas*, both Mayan and *ladino*, who died next to me in combat, the people in the capital who fought for us. They are all dead, but they knew what they were fighting for. My job is to carry on for them. They saw the light at the end of the tunnel so long before I did. It is for me, as one who loved them, to bring that light to our people.

Abram

When I was a young man, all I cared about was money. I did not think at all about the needs of my people, and I did not think at all about my community. My parents had died when I was a small child, so I grew up the hard way, hungry. I started my own business when I was fourteen years old. All I thought about back then was where to get the best prices for my vegetables, where to find cheap transport, how much money was I saving. I was prospering but not thinking. I cared about no one but myself. It took a priest to teach me to love. He was an American priest, Father Stanley Rother, and he lived in my town, Santiago Atitlan.

I did not go to church, so I did not know Father Stanley in my everyday life, and he did not know me. We spoke for the first time in the hospital, after my accident. I had been struck by a car, and suffered serious head injuries and a crushed arm. The hospital took me in and kept me alive, but they would not operate on my arm, because I did not have enough money. I needed surgery and a special implant to replace the ruined bones. It was while I lay in bed, feeling very worried and alone, that Father Stanley came to care for me. He knew only that I was from his parish, and that I was hurt, but he had come all that way just to help me. I did not have to deserve his concern.

He spoke to the administrator, another American, and asked about my surgery. The administrator told him they did not perform such surgeries for Indians, because we could not pay. And this was true. Even with all my savings of so many years of hard labor, I could never pay the price the hospital had asked. I had already resigned myself to the loss of any use of my left arm. But Father Stanley was not resigned. He said that he would take care of the funding, and that his church would pay for everything. And suddenly everything was arranged.

I had my surgery, and the hospital allowed me to stay for many days. The nurses took good care of me, and brought me food, and treated me with kindness. But my eyes were opening at last. I saw the other people, poor like me, on the mats in the corridors, going without the care they needed, suffering, living off the meager food supplies their relatives and friends could bring them. We were the same, and yet treated so differently. I was treated differently because of money. I was treated differently because of Father Stanley's concern. I lay there, thinking for many days about all of this. And I decided that when I left the hospital, I was not going back to my business and I was not going back to money. I was going to serve the church, Father Stanley's church, a church that cared for all of the people.

And this was how I became a catechist. Father Stanley accepted me right away, without a question, almost as though he had been waiting for me, and he put me straight to work. I improved my reading and writing, I studied the Bible, and I helped with the Masses and the religion classes. But most of all, I worked with the people. Together with the other catechists, together with the other villagers, we all worked to try and improve our community. We

preached love and care for one another, we organized village groups for health promotion and literacy and child nutrition. We taught the people to stay
together, to work together, to raise themselves out
of their poverty and suffering by loving and protecting and supporting each other. My life was full. And
the years passed.

I would still be there in Santiago Atitlan if the
army had not come to our town. With them came
the killing and the terror. One by one, members of
our church began to disappear in the night, to be
found later on, murdered with a brutality that
Father Stanley could not bear. Our people have
endured this brutality for five hundred years now,
but Father Stanley was not from our land. He was a
good and kind priest, and had devoted himself to us
for fifteen years, but nothing had prepared him for
this. Perhaps he loved us too much. When I saw the
rage and horror in his face, I worried. I was afraid
for him. When the army called a meeting of all of the
village leaders, I did not want to go. But Father
Stanley was going, and where he went, I went as
well. I could not let him go alone.

The town hall was full when we arrived. The
evangelical ministers were there, the teachers, the
doctors. They sat very stiffly, looking straight ahead.
The soldiers were there, with their big rifles and cartridge belts. The room was very quiet while the military commander said what he had to say. We were
in great danger, he explained to us. The terrorist
guerrillas, the subversives, were everywhere. They
were doing very terrible things. Had we not noticed
the killings, the rapes, the acts of torture? He listed
many barbaric acts that the subversives were doing,

the lies that they were telling to deceive the people. The army had come to the town to protect us, to take care of us. We must report any suspicious activities at once to the military. We must remember that the soldiers were our brothers, here to defend us against the communist threat. Were there any questions? Any comments? Did we have anyone to report?

A minister stood up briefly, and thanked the army for its concern for our safety. He spoke in tight, careful words. The school teachers were silent, looking at their shoes. Then Father Stanley stood up and straightened his shoulders. I knew he could never say anything but the truth, and I knew what was going to happen, but I could do nothing. He spoke calmly, in a strong voice, for everyone to hear. He had been in Santiago Atitlan for fifteen years, he said. Never had there been a killing; never had there been a brutal act before. Only when the army came, had the terror begun. It was the soldiers who raped and tortured and killed. The people had seen them, recognized them. No one was fooled here. The army must stop. The army was acting against the laws of God. And then he sat down. The commander stared, his face red with fury, but we were all allowed to leave.

That night, we met at the parish to plead with Father Stanley to leave Santiago. There was still time, he was a foreigner, we could get him to safety, but he must leave at once. He wouldn't go, though, as I knew he wouldn't. He had been here for so many years. These were his people. He would not leave them in their time of trouble. He would die here if he must, but he would die with them. And so we stopped our pleading with him. We brought him food instead and sat with him through the night, talking about the needs of the people, the village, all the projects we had started with him. We remembered good stories, small triumphs for our people we had managed to win. We spoke of the children, the future, the problems, the army, what to do next. And then we embraced. We all knew it was for the last time. I held him very closely. There were no more words to say. The next day Father Stanley lay dead before his church in the small plaza, cut down by army bullets.

The villagers hurried the other catechists and myself into hiding. I know that some were caught early on and killed, and that others made it out of town. As for me, I spent many nights thinking carefully. The evangelical minister offered me work in another village, helping him preach. But the more I thought of it, the more I knew I could never accept. What good was talk for the people? What kind of parasite would I be, talking and talking, and taking their food? Old friends offered to hide me indefinitely, in their basement, but what good was I to anyone in that way? I had committed my life long ago, back in the hospital, to working for the good of the people. My life was not worth saving if I could no longer serve.

And then I was contacted by members of the resistance. These were people with the same love for the community, the same commitment to serve, as my own. Still, this was a very difficult decision for me. I thought and thought for a long time, and studied my Bible carefully. In the end, it was clear for me what I must do. And so I came to the mountains, to fight. I have been here just short of ten years now. I have kept my commitment.

Elena

Yes, I grew up in a beautiful village, but I did not have a beautiful childhood. This was not because we were poor, though. My family was as well off as the next in our small community. But my father was a drunk and a violent man, and he singled me out for his rages. I have been deaf for as long as I can remember, ever since I was a very small child at least. Perhaps this is why he beat me, but who knows, really, what his reasons were? I may have had some hearing when I was born, but I am not sure of this. One of my earliest memories is the sharp blow to the side of the head he gave me. I think that was when I lost the little hearing I had in my left ear. I remember that things were not the same after that. I do not remember how old I was, but I was old enough to notice the difference.

Since I was deaf, I could not answer when spoken to, and it was hard for me to speak. Perhaps my family thought I was disobedient or wild, or perhaps they were ashamed of me. They did not beat me like my father did, but they never accepted me, either. I did not attend school. I wore the oldest clothing and got the worst scraps of food. The other children, my sisters and cousins, wore shoes—not the leather kind, just the plastic sandals with rubber soles. But they wore shoes while I was always barefooted. And they mocked me. Fortunately, my grandmother saw what was happening to me, and she took me to her house when I was still very young, and kept me there with her. She combed my hair and fed me and gave me the affection and patience I so badly needed. And of course, in return, I loved her totally. Without her, who knows what would have become of me.

By the time I was ten or eleven, my grandmother was growing quite elderly. I had no intention, though, of returning to my family. Whenever we saw each other, they still mocked or mistreated me. Through necessity I had grown into a strong-willed and independent girl. And so I ran away, all alone, to the city of Quetzaltenango, and found myself a job as a housemaid.

I worked for a large *ladino* family there, in a big house with many rooms. My chores included cooking, sweeping and cleaning, going to the market, sewing, and watching over the four small children. Some of these things were new to me, but I watched the others carefully and learned quickly. You do not have to hear to learn. No one in the family seemed to notice how little I spoke. I suppose they thought I spoke only Mayan and had not yet learned Spanish. And what was it to them, after all? I was only their housemaid, not a friend, and I was an *indio* at that. They paid me about ten dollars a month, and my mother would come down from our village every so often to collect my pay. She wasn't angry with me for leaving, and even seemed to respect me a little bit more. As for me, I was content to have food and shelter. A few years passed, and I went back to visit my grandmother and, yes, even the others. After all, they were my own people. Maybe I thought they would see me differently by then. It was so good to see my grandmother, and for a while I was even hopeful about my mother. My father went into a rage on the very first night, but I told him that if he ever beat me again, he would never lay eyes on me for the rest of his life. This seemed to sober him for a bit, and for a few days there was almost peace. I wove and cooked with my mother, and spent some time with my sisters. I could never really find a place for myself there, though. I remember feeling pain as I watched my mother comb my sister's hair and place new red earrings in her ears. In all the years she had received my earnings, she had never given me anything, never fussed over me the way a mother fusses over a daughter, the way she was fussing over my younger sister. I remember the pain I felt, watching them that morning.

All the same, I would probably have stayed there, among our own people, in my own village. I wanted to stay. But my father took to drinking again one night, and he beat me. And just as I had promised, I ran away. This time I ran all the way to the other end of the country, because I had heard that things were better there, and because I was so hurt that I wanted to get as far away from home as possible. I found work again as a maid, only this time on a big *finca*. It was a new place, but my life was about the same. The work was the same, and it lasted all day and late into the night. The pay was about the same, but at least the money was all mine to keep now. And I was determined to start a new life for myself, no matter what. This time things were going to get better. And so they did, but not in the way that I had expected.

There were many other *campesinos* working on this farm. Many were there in search of work, any work, so that they could feed their families, and on the *finca* there was plenty of coffee to pick and corn to tend. Others were there because they were on the run, fleeing the army repression that was sweeping through our country. These people were very careful and spoke little, but as we grew to know and trust each other, we began to tell each other about our lives. We would stay up late at night, in those small thatched huts, talking, me reading their lips by the light of their kerosene lamps. I was learning a lot. One young man, in particular, took the trouble to speak with me slowly, so that I could understand him. Like the others, he simply thought I did not understand Spanish very well, but he was very patient, and treated me always like an intelligent adult. And it was from him that I learned about the uprising in our homeland, about the guerrilla movement. I had heard of this before, of course, but had never really understood what it was all about. But now I was beginning to think about the poverty of our people, the wages we were paid for hard labor, the inequalities. Things were beginning to fit together, to make sense to me.

In the end I ran off to join the guerrilla movement. I was still very young, and didn't know exactly what I was getting myself into. But I knew that these people were good and decent, and I knew that what they were saying about conditions in our country was the truth. I wanted things to get better, not just for me, but for everyone, and I wanted to be part of the change. Really, I was very thrilled about all of this. So I rolled up a blanket and packed some corn tortillas with black beans, and left in the darkness with a young couple I had barely met. Their names were Anna and Geraldo.

It took us nearly two weeks to arrive at the base camp. We left on foot and crossed through the mountains, hiking up and down those steep rocky trails, always hiding from the soldiers, watching for their traces. We got lost a few times, which was frightening, but somehow Geraldo always found the markers we were looking for, the trees with the strange root formations, the big rock at the edge of the waterfall. I was tired from all the walking, but very happy. It made me happy to be seeing my own country in this new way, to be seeing all its green beauty, but through new eyes.

When we finally arrived, I had quite a shock. We were suddenly in a small sheltered area surrounded by a dozen *compañeros* in olive green uniforms, all of them armed with rifles and machetes. For the first time I felt frightened and insecure, for somehow I had failed to imagine this part of my new life. At the *finca*, the *compas* had worn civilian clothing, of course, and had carried no weapons. The sight of so many strangers, so serious and so heavily armed brought tears to my eyes. But Anna was there, and she seemed to understand what was happening and hurried me off to a tent to rest and have some food. She sat with me there until late into the night, comforting me, sewing a uniform so that it would fit me better, promising to teach me to read and write. I finally fell asleep next to her, exhausted.

My new life of course, was not easy, but this did not trouble me much. My old life had not been easy either. Here at least I was treated as an equal, and as a sister. I came to love the other *compañeros* very much for this. But I never told them of my deafness.

Heeding the Call to Action

Don't ask me why, perhaps I was afraid of losing their respect. I hid it for as long as I could, allowing them to try to teach me more Spanish, watching the others at all times to make sure I was not missing anything. But in the end, of course, they did find me out. They had sent me up to the hill top for my night shift at guard duty, a job which always terrified me since, in the darkness, I am quite helpless. When the shift ended, Anna came up to take my place, approaching me from behind. She saw me leaning forward, staring intently into the darkness, but when she called out my name, I didn't answer. She tried several more times, louder and louder, but still I did not answer. Only when she touched my shoulder, did I start, obviously unaware that she had been standing so close to me. And so she knew, finally, that I could not hear—not her voice, not anything, really.

And so the *compañeros* had to send me down from the mountains, despite my desperate pleading that they let me stay. I knew they were right, of course. No one can survive up there if they can't hear the enemy coming after them, or a shout of warning in the night. I would have been killed there. It was just a matter of time. But still, it broke my heart to leave. In those few months, I had come to feel part of a new family, one that respected and cared for me, and I did not want to lose this. I understand now, that it was their love for me that sent me away. And in the end, not only did they save my life, but they gave me a better one.

I wanted to continue with the *compañeros*, so I was transferred to one of our support structures. I ended up working in an underground house where the wounded *compas* stay, recovering from their injuries. My job is to run the household, really, to see to the foods and the chores, to make sure the *compas* have paper and pens for their studies, to talk with them and to attend their needs. I have two hearing aids now, one for each ear, so I can finally really hear and speak. I can have conversations now. Do you know what this means to me? And I no longer have to hide my deafness. There is no more shame. That man over there, Adam, he is my *compa* now. You see the furniture he is making? Take a closer look at his right hand. It is plastic. Had you noticed? I think it was watching him make the furniture for this house, seeing him always so high-spirited, always teasing, that drew me to him. And so finally, yes, I am happy. I have always felt that I can do more than survive. I have much to give, to contribute. At last there is a way for me.

Gabriel

Ah, God, the Karl Marx question! I knew it. You foreigners are all alike, you all ask the same questions. You think you can get a handle on us, understand us better, by finding out if we consider ourselves to be Marxists. But look, even if I could figure out how to answer that question, you're missing the whole point of what is going on in our country.

Here, have some of this great mango here, or a little avocado, while I try to explain. One thing for sure, this part of the world produces great fruit, don't you think? Our lands are so rich and yet our people are so poor.

Personally, I feel that Karl Marx was a very great man, and a very important thinker for his day and age. I'm one of the lucky ones in Guatemala, I was able to attend the university and get hold of some his materials to read. I think the man had a very interesting and original mind. Many of his concepts overlap with some of the traditional ways of life in my own country. Have you spent much time with the Mayan peoples? Have you been to their villages? So you saw how they are, then, how they stick together and take care of each other, how the whole community shares so many things. They have a very strong communal streak. They always have. So do the Amish peoples in your country, I hear. So did the early Christians. Were they Marxist? I don't think, somehow, that old Karl has a monopoly on these ideas. The same goes for the notion that people should be able to work collectively and share in the benefits. Don't you people have food co-ops in your country? Labor unions? Do we have to give up our cultural heritage to make everyone happy with us?

Look, Marx had a lot of ideas. We will probably disagree on some and coincide on others, especially if they are concepts that would fit well into our own, modern-day conditions. But coinciding on certain issues doesn't make us zombie-like followers of Mr. Marx. We have minds of our own, a country of our own, problems and issues of our own. To label us so superficially is to rob us of our individuality, of our own thinking. In many ways, I see this as a problem of cultural racism. Up in the mountains, our platoons are 90 percent Mayan. Do you think those people are all up there because of some nineteenth-century European?

More importantly, your question focuses all the attention on only one aspect of our struggle. Let me tell you why I am in the revolution here. I am not risking my life to make *das Kapital* into the new Bible. I am fighting because in my country child malnutrition is close to 85 percent. Ten percent of all children will be dead before the age of five, and that is only the number actually reported to government agencies. Close to 70 percent of our people are functionally illiterate. There is almost no industry in our country—you need land to survive. Less than 3 percent of our landowners own over 65 percent of our lands. In the last fifteen years or so, there have been over 150,000 political murders and disappearances. That is why I am up here, fighting, even now that I am so old my knees want to give out.

Don't talk to me about Gandhi; he wouldn't have survived a week here. Do you know the history of our peaceful reform efforts here? I once worked in a union, but after a march one day my friends were found dead in a gutter rolled up in their banners. Do you know how many unionists have died? Look at the Indian rights movement. The CUC leaders were burned alive in the Spanish Embassy. The rural health promoter campaign? Those people are dead. The church efforts to form co-ops and self-help networks for the poor? Well, those people were all accused of communism too, don't you see? So many priests have been killed here—I don't want to think of how many of their catechists. There was a peaceful movement for progress here, once. They were crushed. We were crushed. For Gandhi's methods to work, there must be a government capable of shame. We lack that here.

After it is all over I would like to have a family. I would like to work a small garden and maybe start some hydroelectric energy systems in our rural areas. There's no electricity but there's plenty of running water. My *compa* wants to do rural health organizing. All of us have ideas, plans, on how to make our country a place where everyone can live, not just the rich. We would like to struggle into the twentieth century without having to pay with our lives. As I said, I feel that Karl Marx was a fine man, but he died in industrialized Germany over a hundred years ago without ever setting foot in Guatemala. What did he know of our history, our conditions, our people? What did he know of our indigenous population? Please, tell all of your friends, tell them to just think of us as what we are, as Guatemalan citizens and revolutionaries. What is it about foreigners that they can only comprehend us by how close we come to fitting some European precedent? Why are we, as just ourselves, so invisible?

Gaspar

So our stories have made you sad, you tell me. Yes, this I can understand, my friend, but tears are not the right response. For every painful story there is one of beauty, one to learn from. Here, let me give you a big bear hug and sit you down near the fire, and we'll have a long talk. What will it be now, a gin and tonic? Or some of our good coffee? You must eat too, and tell me what you have been thinking. I want to hear all about your experiences. But first, please, let me serve you some of this good soup. You must never forget the art of enjoyment. Otherwise the pain of survival will crush you. We have seen hard times, it is true. When Everardo first joined us so many years ago, we were only nine in number. He became our tenth *compañero*. We were only just starting out, back then, a small secret group, trying to organize a popular base, trying to prepare for a future that we knew would be very difficult. We had virtually no supplies at all. I can remember when our total organizational assets sank to three tamales and about forty cents. You laugh, but it is true. We were very definitely a poor people's army from the very beginning. I can tell you this with some ruefulness.

It was always the villagers, the local people, who pulled us through. From the start they were with us, with their trust and their generosity. You have met Celia, yes? The one with the sweet face. She is an excellent military strategist and a promising young officer. I have known her since she was a very small girl, when her mother used to send her to us with food supplies. Both she and her brother joined our ranks as soon as they were old enough. He died in combat many years ago, and she is now the old-timer up in our volcanoes, the experienced leader for the younger ones to turn to. I am proud of this woman, as I would be of my own daughter, as I am proud of so many others like her. There are times when I feel like a proud, old grandfather, watching this new generation, the children of our *compañeros*, fighting at our sides. So many of my own generation have already given their lives. Of those of us from so many years ago, Everardo is one of only a few left alive with me.* The others, who were so much more than brothers, fell one by one in the early years. Yes, those were times of pain, very terrible pain. But you must have the right perspective. So many very special people have been lost to us. You must learn to focus, not on the tragedy of their deaths, but on the magnificence of their lives. This is what they would have wished.

For the first eight years of our existence, we organized in total secrecy. Did you know that? We wished to avoid army repression against our supporters, until we were strong enough to protect our people. So we worked clandestinely for years, strengthening our relations with the villagers, clarifying our own political positions, training new members, and arranging for food and medical supply networks. All this time, we never announced our existence as a new organization. We knew we had to be ready for the army before we could become pub-

*Everardo was captured in combat by the army in March, 1992, and at this writing is being tortured in a clandestine prison.

licly known. We knew we would need great strength for what was to come. And so we were patient, very patient.

It was in those early days that the Mayan villagers, especially, confirmed our beliefs that it would be the rural poor who would play a key role in our revolution, and that equal rights for the Mayan race must be a basic tenet of any political platform. We could see for ourselves what these people were suffering and how they were abused and cast aside by our society as if they were not people at all. And we could see for ourselves the remarkable unity and courage that they possessed. It was these people who brought us food and medicines in the early years, despite their own poverty. It was these people who risked their own lives protecting us, and who sent their sons and daughters to fight with us. Did you know that in all those years of secrecy, not one villager ever turned us in to the army, despite the dangers we represented? In those eight long years, there was not one betrayal. I will never forget this. We must never forget this.

I remember in the very early days, being worried that the villagers would perhaps not accept us. I had great faith in these communities. After all, that is why I had come to this area in the first place. I was not interested in leading a small band of city intellectuals. And yet, what had these people ever known from outsiders, except abuse and exploitation? I knew that our first encounters would be very important, and I had the highest of hopes. We were camped far up in the mountains, in the dense green foliage, but day by day we would come out and approach the communities, to speak with the people and explain why we were there. In the beginning they would listen very courteously, offering us food and water, but no comments. Then, as they came to know us, they began to ask questions, to raise new ideas, to hold discussions with us. They were still noncommittal in their relations with us, although friendly and generous, and I knew we were being closely observed. I was happy when the village elders began to sit with us through the long afternoons, listening, suggesting, contemplating.

One day the village priest came to speak with me. By priest I do not refer to a man of the Catholic church. This was a priest of the old, Mayan beliefs, which our people have managed to preserve, despite the brutality of the conquest, over the last five centuries. This priest was not a large man, nor was he young, but he had great dignity and intelligence. As he spoke with me late into the evening, I knew that I was being examined, considered. He was weighing my sincerity and my character. He spoke to me the next day and the next, and finally, he asked that I accompany him on a brief journey.

We set out just before dawn the following day, only the two of us. He led the way on the narrow rocky paths, straight up along the sharp ridge of the volcano. The climb was a steep one, and the air was crisp and cold. As we walked, I could see the morning mists far below us begin to drift upwards, as if to follow our trail. I felt no hunger, only eagerness and curiosity. I had no idea where we were going, but this didn't disturb me in the least. I had complete faith in the slight and solitary figure of the priest leading me onwards. I understood that I would learn our destination soon enough. Everything in its time.

Heeding the Call to Action

By midday we had arrived at a crescent of large stones hidden deep in the trees. Although battered, it was clear from their shape that they had been formed by human hands, some long time ago. My friend stopped, and stood in the center of the arc, motioning me forward to his side. I cannot tell you why, but as I started towards him, I knew that I was on holy ground, and I felt very moved. And we were, indeed, in such a place, for before us stood a small altar. We had come to a place of prayer and offerings, built by the Mayans many hundreds of years ago. It is a secret place now, the knowledge of its meaning and location handed down by their descendants from generation to generation, its existence guarded from the world of tourism and exploitation. There are many such secret places here in our country. Somehow—I do not know how—these people were able not only to physically survive the conquest, but to preserve their old ways too, their faith, their arts, their languages, their dignity.

As I knelt with my friend, he began to chant his prayers, his eyes half closed, his arms relaxed. He seemed so very serene. As he prayed, I saw that others had quietly entered as well. They seemed unperturbed to find me there and unpacked their offerings, laying them out neatly upon the altar: foods, corn, coins, colored bottles filled with liquids. Soon the air was filled with the quiet chants, each person speaking confidently with the spirit of his choice. Small and ragged, most of them gaunt with malnutrition, they were in clear repose, secure in the knowledge that this holy place belonged to them. As I watched, the priest pulled out a small flask, drinking half and handing me the rest, then returning to the concentration of his prayers. The others drank too, and for a long while there was only the sound of the chanting, the clinking of the drinking flasks, and the wind. When it was all over, the priest explained quietly that he had prayed for our safety, and for the success of our struggle, which was also their struggle. Then he placed a small amulet around my neck, fastening it securely. This was to keep me from all harm and evil.

I have never forgotten that day. It is one of my most special memories. But it is tinged with sadness also. Not long afterwards, the priest was seized by the army and tortured to death. He died in a very terrible way, but I will not tell you how. He knew exactly where I was staying at the time of his capture, but he never said a word, never betrayed me at all. For this reason, I am still alive, and he is long dead, this man who would have been so close a friend. But even with his death, and even with the wave of terror that followed, the villagers stayed with us. They did more than accept us, they became the revolution.

How many stories of heroism I could tell you. But it is not the heroism of these times that I consider to be the true treasure here. There is something deeper and more moving still, and that is the way that all of us, no matter what our race or class, were able to stay together, trust one another, protect and love each other despite our great differences. It is from these experiences that so much hope has flowered for me.

Jennifer

For me, it all started out in the United States. Don't laugh, it's true. I was doing some volunteer work over at the local refugee center. After all, my grandparents were refugees, so it seemed like an all-American thing for me to do. And this was back when the Statue of Liberty was being renovated. Remember all the hoopla about her? Forgive my cynicism, but maybe after you hear my stories, you will understand me better.

At first I worked with all kinds of refugees, people from Africa and Asia, the Caribbean, Latin America. I loved the work and the people, and they were teaching me a great deal about what was really going on in the Third World. I had always been fascinated with international politics and would stay up late into the night, poring over files and historical accounts, trying to work out difficult petitions and presentations. For a long time it was an enjoyable activity, a fine puzzle to be put together, a public service to good people. But it was, in the end, just a hobby, an intellectual exercise. My first Guatemala case changed this forever.

The *Guatemaltecos* did not arrive one by one. They arrived, characteristically, as a small community and moved en masse into a small poor neighborhood not far from the Center. When a few of the people decided to seek political asylum, the whole group decided to apply at the same time, turning our tiny office into chaos in a single afternoon. We had little information about Guatemala, too few typewriters, and the various members of the group spoke several different dialects of Mayan, for which we had no interpreter. Like I said, chaos. In the end though, we all had a good time. The women in the group took over and began sharing the food they had brought with them, and some crayons and coloring books were found for the children. We managed to piece together some conversations in Spanish, at which both sides were a bit sketchy. Add a few soft drinks, and we were on our way. By the end of the afternoon, we at least understood who these people were and where they were from. We also knew that they were in very desperate trouble. Once they had all packed up and left together, we could only stare at each other and shake our heads.

As time went on, we were able to flesh out their histories. These people were survivors, representing bits and pieces of different destroyed communities from their homelands. It was not easy for them to tell their stories, but they tried, giving us a new chunk of information with each visit. Daily we listened to stories of burning villages, murderous army sweeps, a proud indigenous population being driven ruthlessly towards extinction. They showed us the scars on their bodies, the carefully guarded photographs of the dead. We watched their children run for cover, weeping at the sound of any loud noises, especially helicopters. Somewhere in Mexico these different survivors had found each other and regrouped into a new, patchwork community, and had moved on together to *El Norte*, hoping to find survival here. Every day we listened to these stories, and every day we became more committed to these battered, gentle people.

Heeding the Call to Action

You might think that with stories like these, their asylum cases would have been a piece of cake, right? After all, wealthy Russian ballet stars get it all the time. But a person can only get asylum in the U. S. if he or she comes from a communist country. If you come from a country backed by our government, then you have no "reasonable fear of persecution" no matter what happened to you. This is not what the law says, but is nonetheless the reality of our justice system. Amnesty International listed Guatemala as one of the worst human rights violators in the western hemisphere back then. Did this make any difference to the immigration courts? Hell no. Excuse me, but these really are bitter memories. Over and over again, I watched the bureaucrats discard stories because they were too "old" or did not have any authentication. Scars were found to be of unclear origin. Psychiatric evaluation of the children's grim drawings were discounted as unreliable. According to the courts, these people were here simply to make money. They wanted citizenship in this great country of ours so that they could make a lot of money and have fancy cars. Therefore, they had made up these tall tales to help get a foot through the door. Now it was time for them to go home.

Home? The rest of us would stare at each other in amazement as the preliminary rulings were handed down. We filed appeals, an edge of panic coming into the work. A friendly office lost a case, and their client was deported. He was found decapitated a week later, his battered body lying in a pool of blood in a city gutter. Our panic deepened. The Guatemalans, though, remained quite calm, talking among themselves, working out emergency plans for what to do next. I caught one of the older men watching me once with a half smile on his face, as if he were amused by my childlike sense of betrayal. The other refugees seemed to feel the same way. Why were we all so surprised at being badly treated by a government agency? What was all the fuss about? What had we expected?

As the new hearing dates grew closer, we ransacked libraries for new materials. But there was so little published. Think about it, have you ever read a serious article in *Newsweek* about Guatemala? Me either. And yet there are an estimated 100,000 children missing one or both parents in the two northwest indigenous states alone. There are only eight million people in the total Guatemalan population. How do you prove that a village has been wiped out? By calling up the generals and asking them if they really did it? If the survivors are not credible, who is? The dead? And so that was how I got the idea of going and finding some information myself. I could testify. I am a U. S. citizen, I'm over forty years of age, and I have two degrees from Ivy League Universities. Who's going to tell me I'm making up stories so I can get a green card and make a lot of money? I was making a lot more money before I started all this volunteer work.

And so I packed. I had decided on Mexico, since the largest refugee camps were there. I figured that this would be the quickest and easiest way to collect some testimonies. The people would all be in one place and out from under the watchful eyes of the soldiers. Within Guatemala I wouldn't know even where to start. Unlike El Salvador, no human rights offices were permitted to operate there. Not even the International Red Cross was allowed into the country at that time. Mexico sounded a lot easier, but it wasn't.

I landed in Chiapas, the Mexican province bordering Guatemala, on the same day that a roving band of Guatemalan soldiers crossed into Mexican territory and rampaged through one of the refugee camps. A pregnant woman was left dead in a cornfield, hacked open at the belly. Her little son lay at her side, his amputated genitals stuffed into his dead mouth. The hysterical survivors had been rushed into small neighboring Mexican communities until a safer place could be arranged for them. The Mexican government, with its collapsing economy, feared any military confrontations at its borders, and ordered the transfer of all the camps to the Yucatan area. The refugees did not want to move so far from their beloved homelands, despite the dangers. A crackdown began. The church got involved. All foreigners were thrown out of the region. Journalists were being deported. That was the week I arrived for some easy information.

I'm not sure exactly how I ended up getting into the camps. It took nearly ten days of waiting and having doors slammed in my face. People were frightened and angry, and the government agencies were everywhere. No one wanted anything at all to do with a *gringa*, believe me. But I just hung around and hung around and basically refused to leave until someone gave up and agreed to help me. I cannot tell you who this was because she is still there, and has already taken enough flack. She doesn't need any more. But I hope that someday she reads this and finds out how much her trust meant to me.

Getting to the village where the refugees were was also something of an adventure. I had no pass to get into the area, so someone had to drive me in at night, stuffed behind some sacks in the back of a pickup. As we drew near the main checkpoint, the driver pulled over and pointed to a young Mexican *campesina* at the side of the road. He told me to go with her, and quickly, but to be sure not to walk too far, as the border was only five kilometers away. Then, laughing, he took off again, leaving me with the pretty, feisty-looking teenager. Her name was Magdalena, and she wasted no time taking charge of me. She checked to be sure I was wearing decent walking shoes, then grabbed my hand and started pulling me down a narrow trail, giggling at the phenomenal amount of noise I seemed to be able to make. It was dark out, but the walk was beautiful all the same, up and down through shadowed green hills, as angular and steep as the cliffs in a Japanese ink drawing.

When we reached the edge of the village it was late at night. Magdalena stopped and told me to wait beneath a cluster of trees while she told the rest of the people of my arrival. She ran on ahead then, and rang a large gong in the center of a small clearing. As I watched, the village came abruptly to life, people stumbling out of their low, thatched huts, rubbing their eyes warily, clutching their children. They spoke among themselves briefly, then motioned me forward to a small stump that served as a chair. A steaming tin cup of coffee appeared, and some corn tortillas were placed silently before me by a woman with battered brown hands and a limp. A large kerosene lamp was lit. As I stared at the circle of people around me, they stared back, and I felt a jolt of recognition. They were so much like the clients back home, and so unlike any other people I had ever known. I recognized those startling, tilted eyes and the tiny body frames that spoke worlds of hard labor and malnutrition. I recognized the double woven cloths, covered with Mayan symbols, wrapping the restless babies. And I recognized the looks on their faces, the fear and distrust mixing with a determination to hear me out, to give me a fair chance to say whatever I had come to say. A very old man stepped forward, and gave me the flowery speech of welcome that their collective good manners required.

Sitting on the low stump, I explained to them why I had come to the camp, and asked for their help. They conferred quickly with each other, and asked questions for a while about the refugee situation in the United States, watching me closely as I spoke, nodding politely at my responses. Finally a younger woman motioned to my tape recorder, and another small stump was hauled over to my side. A man with graying hair and an uncertain expression sat down on it, looking anxiously into my face. I reached out to shake hands, not knowing how else to greet him, and saw that his own were trembling badly. Two women crowded close behind him, touching his shoulder, handing him food that he had not asked for. This man, I was told, had a story that would help us. As he began, the others stood stoically in a circle around us, arms crossed, alert.

He was from a village, a medium-sized village, the man explained to me. Maybe 300 people lived there, all of them Mayan, all of them trying to scratch a living together from their mountainous land. It was a hard life and they were all poor, but they loved the land, and they were true to their own culture. Their language was Canjobal. The man was born and raised in the village, as were his father and grandfather, his wife and his children. None of them had ever thought of leaving, even when the army arrived in their region. They knew they would be in for some hard times, as trouble always accompanied the army. But to leave their own lands, their ancestral homelands, was unthinkable.

But things grew even worse than they had expected. Dead bodies began to appear in the roads. People—good people—disappeared in the night. There was torture, such terrible things were beginning to happen. The man's voice became unsteady as he spoke, and the other villagers began to fuss over him, draping a shawl about his shoulders, lacing his coffee with liquor from a cracked green bottle. I watched his hands, still trembling so that he could barely handle his tin mug, and realized, with a start, that he was not as old as he looked. His hair had prematurely whitened.

The troops began to come more often to their village, he explained. They were angry and accusatory, always searching for the "subversives." Finally, one day a large group of soldiers arrived all together, in big trucks and with machine guns. It was early afternoon, so some of the people were away tending the cornfields, or gone to the market. But the rest were ordered into the village square. He had hoped that the soldiers were only going to give them a lecture, a warning that they must never assist the guerrillas, but even as he prayed for this, he knew that they were in very bad trouble. He knew this from the soldiers' faces. They were glassy-eyed and wild, shoving people into the square as if they were corralling cattle. The children were crying. An old woman fell, and was jerked ungraciously to her feet. His heart sank when the soldiers, cursing, forced all of the men into the small town hall at gun point, clubbing those who resisted. The people cried out that they had done nothing, that they were not the guerrillas, but no one would listen, and no one would explain anything.

Inside the building, the man could barely breathe, from the crush of people against him, and from his own terror. Gunfire began, and the screams of the women as they were torn away from their children. The women were all shot. Some were killed outright, others dragged off and raped before being murdered. Some of the men tried to break out through the door, but the machine guns were there, waiting. After awhile, a very long while, there were no more women's voices, only the hysterical weeping of the children in the square.

And then it was the children's turn to die. But not by gunfire. The soldiers wasted no bullets on them. They were dragged out one by one and disemboweled. The soldiers took out long knives and cut out their stomachs. They opened the doors to the hall now and then, so that the men could see what was happening. They yelled that the children were the seeds of the subversives, that they had been born with the subversive sickness. The man watched in horror. All the children died that afternoon. He could not save even one. After a while, he just crouched in the corner and waited for his own death, hoped for his own death. He could bear no more. As he told this part of the story, one of the women hurried up to him and placed her small, rosy child on his lap to hold. He hardly seemed to notice, though. The other villagers, weeping openly, huddled close to him, trying to give him the strength to finish his story. I barely had the strength to listen.

In the end, only the men of his village were left, and they, too, were dragged out one by one to have their throats slit. There was little struggle now. But still, it took so long for so many to die. In the end, the soldiers grew tired and tossed a grenade into the hallway to finish off the last of them. The man awoke a long time later, under a pile of bodies. There was one other dazed survivor, staring at him from across the room, staring at his own blood soaked clothing. The soldiers were still outside, laughing and eating a cow they had slaughtered, the bodies of the villagers scattered around them. The other man tried to escape into the darkness, but the soldiers heard his boots on the ground and fired after him. So he, himself, did not try to escape. He just lay back down among the corpses and waited till the soldiers were gone. Then he removed his shoes, running barefooted through the piled corpses, into the woods, into the mountains and far away, all the way to Mexico. There had been no one left in his family to stay for.

I stared into this man's face. He was tearful, but his gaze was steady enough. It was the good, decent face of a *campesino*, born to hard labor and traditional family values. It was a guileless face, filled with pain. He stared back at me, as if hoping for some explanation, some idea or thought that would make it all clear. Finding none, he asked me to pray with him. The other villagers crowded around us, and together, in the lamplight, we all prayed aloud. They asked for nothing else.

That was not the only story I heard that night, but it is the only one I am going to tell you right now. Really, it is enough, isn't it? The others were survivors, too, some even from the same village. The two young school teachers at the camp were from there, but had been visiting their sister in another village that day. The others had all left the same way, barefoot and running, fleeing different regions but the same terror. In Mexico they had quickly organized themselves. Those who could read would teach; those who knew some medicine would try to organize a makeshift clinic. The elders would speak for the group. And so they were surviving. They sent messages of support to the refugees in my country, wishing them strength and well-being.

Back home, I sat in my office and thought for a long time. I found a document written by a priest who had interviewed the same man with the graying hair. He had given his story not long after arriving at the camp. Word for word, it read the same—no embellishments, no contradictions, no changes. When a photographer came through town, I questioned him closely about this region. Yes, he had been there; yes, he had heard of this village. He had even gone to see the place, to check it out. No one would go with him; no one would go near this place, so it took him a while, but he did find it. He found the burned remains of a town hall in the middle of a weed-covered clearing. Next to that was the charred roof of what must have been the church, the blackened crucifix was still there. And nearby, the bones of the dead. He had started to take a photograph, but then, awed, he had put his camera away and knelt to pray, instead.

And so I packed up my office and handed in my letter of resignation. It was time to go to Guatemala and find out what on earth was going on, and what could be done about it. As I packed, I wondered about the guerrilla movement, too. Who were these people? Why were they fighting? And why was the army so threatened that it would go to such terrible lengths to stop them?

PART II
Life
in the Revolution

Note

The following stories describe life in the early stages of the revolution, and the personal adjustments encountered by those newly-arrived in the mountains. Conditions were very difficult: the compañeros faced inadequate supplies of food, warm clothing, basic equipment, and, more ominously, weapons and ammunition. The army, equipped with helicopters, planes, bombs, mortars, machine guns, and ground transport, ruthlessly hunted them, torturing and killing those even suspected of supplying or aiding them. The situation was little better in the capital, where the urban underground came close to extermination. One by one, the clandestine houses fell, their inhabitants tortured until they revealed the locations of yet other houses and meeting places.

Most compañeros did not expect to survive to see the triumph, but simply hoped that by giving their lives, they would place it within the reach of the younger generation. They envisioned themselves as a bridge.

Florecita

Life was so hard for us, in the beginning, up there in the mountains. Conditions were so difficult. It was not just the cold, or the sadness from being so far away from our homes and our loved ones. It was that we were a new army, a poor people's army, lacking in so many basic supplies. The government troops were everywhere, hunting us down, killing anyone they could find who dared to bring us food or medicines. We needed backpacks; we needed clothing and blankets; we needed food and weapons; we needed everything. Back then we lost some people, not because they did not want to stay with us, but because we could not even give them a rifle and a pair of boots. They had to go back to their villages for a while, if they could, or else to Mexico for a few years. They are back here with us now. Things have changed so much. Do you know what it does to my old timer's heart to see those people return to us, to fight with us, now that the conditions have made it possible? To know that they never gave up hope for our struggle?

I remember once we had been without enough food for a very long time. The army had been bombarding our area of the volcano, and no one had made it through with supplies of any kind. Little by little, though, things grew quieter, and a few of us were sent out to hunt for food. We were to bring back roots, berries, herbs, small animals, anything that we could find or catch, and we left with big sacks to fill as best we could. We climbed down the steep side of the mountain slowly, combing the whole region, but there was little to find. Because of the war, most civilians had fled the area. To be too close to us could call down army suspicion on them, whether they were helping us or not. We found a few ears of corn left growing in a burned cornfield and some tasty roots along the bank of a nearby river. The charred remains of an old farmhouse lay at the edge of the cornfield, but the ruins yielded no supplies. I was standing there, wondering sadly who the inhabitants had been, and where they had gone, when I heard a faint noise in the bushes nearby. It was a poor old cow, very thin with matted fur full of twigs and brambles.

Thin as she was, this cow really made our day. She meant food, and not just any food, but much-needed protein for the entire camp. We were so proud of this cow. She was in bad shape, so it took us several days to drag her back up the volcano, and on the way up we gave her greens to eat, and tried to clean up her fur a bit. We tried to make her look good. It made us all a little homesick, sitting around a small fire at night, and brushing out her fur, talking to her. She really was a very sweet cow, too. She had an especially nice personality—very affectionate, like a pet. So of course, by the time we got her all the way back to the camp, there was no way we were going to eat her. It took quite a bit of talking, but after awhile, we convinced everyone that the best thing for all of us was to keep her for her milk. And in the end, everyone agreed, because she really was a very nice cow. We named her Flora, or Florecita, and she stayed with us for quite a while.

Anita
in the Mountains

So where did we finish up last time? With my decision to leave for the mountains, right? Well I got there just fine. I learned to climb and shoot and carry my weight in supplies—I loved it, really. Physically it wasn't all that hard for me to adapt, since I'm a strong woman anyway, and I'd spent that year in medical school doing my residency in the jungle, remember? At least, I didn't arrive in the mountains as a hot house flower. What was really hard for me was learning to find my way around, since I grew up in a city. I got lost all the time, no matter how hard I tried. The other *compas* thought this was pretty funny, but they really worked to teach me and encourage me. No one ever made fun of me. They would just point out a certain tree with strange branches and tell me to remember it as my marker. But really now, a tree? We were living in the woods!

I loved my work. I was the unit physician, but I was also responsible for physical fitness programs in the morning and for political education. The fitness program was often comical, especially when we got some macho young *compas* straight in from the city. I would always tell them to take it easy the first few days, to take things gradually and build up their bodies with time. But of course, they would always want to keep up with the women, even those of us who had been up there for months and months. After a heavy session of squats and abdominals, let alone the mountain climbing it takes just to get from tent to tent, it was not unusual to see some proud newcomer limping around sheepishly for a few days. But you must never laugh at a beginner. They learned for themselves, just as they learned that cooking and sewing and washing were no longer only women's work. All of us had a lot to learn, or unlearn, up there in the mountains.

It was the political work that I loved the best. We would all sit together in a big circle and talk about our heritage, the conquest, the problems of land distribution in our country, the racism. Most of our people were Maya from small villages, taught since birth that they were inferior. My goal, in teaching, was to convince them that they counted, that they had equal value, that they had much to say and much to give. My goal was to tell them that the new world, after our triumph, would be theirs. My reward was the expression on their faces. And you should hear the things they had to say, once they believed that they would be listened to with respect. So many ideas, so much wisdom these gentle people had stored up in their minds. Our country will be in good hands, some day. This much I know.

I would have stayed up in the mountains forever. I was happy enough with my work and my life, even though it was dangerous and often sad. I was in love with another young *compa*, Mario. We fought side by side in combat, and we could talk about anything. He had little formal education, but was very intelligent, and respected women as revolutionaries and as equals. He was very quiet and kindly, and completely dedicated. That is why we are not together now. When I was hurt later on, he could have stayed in the city with me while I recovered. But he chose to go back to combat. He knew how much he was needed in the mountains, and so that was the end of that. I respected his decision and I still do, but that doesn't mean it wasn't painful at the time. Most of the story I am going to tell you now is about painful memories, but I want to tell it anyway. I want you to write about it for us.

The day I was shot started out like any other day. I was on kitchen duty that morning, washing pots at the edge of the river. Some other *compas* were swimming nearby, getting cleaned up after hauling supplies from the bottom of the volcano, splashing water at me. What we didn't know was that one of our new people, a young *compa* named Marcelino, had slipped away during the night to head back towards his village. He had a serious alcoholism problem which he had not told us about, and in a moment of despair, he had decided he could not handle the situation, and had left all alone. We would have escorted him down, to safety, but he had been too ashamed to tell us of his problem. He did not get far before the army caught and tortured him, and it did not take long to make him talk. I am sorry for him, when I think of this. He only wanted to go home. Instead he met a bad death and almost took the rest of us with him.

I was bending over a large iron cauldron when the first hail of bullets hit us. It took me completely by surprise. I heard the explosion of gunfire, from so many, many guns and saw a river of blood pouring from my face. For a moment, I couldn't feel much and was able to crawl to safety behind some big rocks at the river's edge. Our *compas* had appeared instantly on the ledge above us, and fought back against the soldiers with so much strength that we were protected. It is thanks to them that I and the others in the river that day were neither killed nor captured. I lay behind the rocks for a long time while they fought. The bullet had taken off the right half of my jaw, and I was bleeding heavily, but all I could do was wrap up my face in the bandana I had been wearing and lie still. I knew the injury was very serious, and thought I would probably die, except that it hurt like hell. I had always been told that when you are truly close to death, there is no pain. So I lay there feeling cheated and mad—mad that not only was I going to die, but that this "no pain" stuff was just an old fairy tale. The worst part, though, was listening to the other wounded ones crying out for help. I was their doctor, but I couldn't even move a finger to help them. I could only lie there and listen, and wonder who was hurt, and how badly. This was the worst.

The battle went on for a long time, but I don't know how long. I fainted off and on, but I lived through it. I woke up to the sound of someone whispering my name nearby, and I tossed some pebbles to attract their attention. Then I saw the anxious faces of my friends leaning over me, gentle hands pulling me upright, checking my body for other injuries. People had seen me go down and thought I had been shot through the head, so they were really happy to find me not only alive but conscious, as well. They hauled me away from the river back to a hiding place where the rest of the *compas* were waiting. Our situation was very bad—the scouts had returned with information about the army. Intent on wiping us out once and for all, they had encircled our mountain peak with several thousand foot soldiers. Helicopters were flying overhead, strafing the area. We could hear the explosions from where we were hiding. There were seventy of us.

My mind began to clear as we sat listening. A *compa* brought me my medical bag, cleaning and bandaging my face as best she could. I gave myself an injection of antibiotics. My hands were working perfectly well, even though I was dizzy, so I turned to the others. There were three wounded people besides me, two with wounds through the leg, which I quickly cleaned and bandaged. The third was harder. A young woman, Alicia, had taken a piece of shrapnel in the head. Part of her skull had been torn off, but she was alive. All I could do was bandage her very carefully and give her antibiotics. She was semi-conscious but didn't know where she was, and kept crying out, which made it very dangerous for all of us. We built a rough stretcher for her and covered her to keep her warm. It was all we could do. We carried her out of the mountains that way, with her head wrapped in a flimsy bandage.

The others talked quietly for a while and came up with the best plan they could. The vanguard would go ahead and find the weakest parts of the circle, the smallest breaks, and signal us to follow. We would move only at night and hide during the daytime. This would mean climbing down the most treacherous parts of the volcano, the steepest cliffs, in the dark. But we had no choice at all. We left right then, moving without even the help of our flashlights. Two of the wounded were carried. The other compa and I could walk, so long as we were supported by a friend. You ask how I could walk with that kind of injury? As a doctor I can only answer that I don't know. As a *compa*, I can tell you that you never know what you are capable of until the time comes. Then you do what you have to do. And so I walked.

It took us ten days to get out of the mountains. There are many parts of this journey that I can't remember. So much is blurry. I think there were times when I blacked out altogether, and was carried. But mostly I remember walking and walking, leaning on Chabelita, the *compa* assigned to help me. She was very young and very strong, and even though she was new to the mountains, she was calm and disciplined. She did everything for me that she could. I remember cursing the cold wind because it hurt my face so much, and drinking river water and rice water through some old IV tubes from my medical bag. I could eat nothing with my destroyed jaw. Alicia was in very bad condition, but there was so little I could do to help her. She survived in the end, but I do not know how.

The soldiers were everywhere, hunting us, shouting, dropping explosives from helicopters overhead. Sometimes they passed very near to our hiding places—so near that we would be reaching for our weapons, expecting our final battle. Mario was in the vanguard, searching for safe routes out of the volcano, so I saw little of him. During our nighttime marches he was far ahead, and often during the days he was away on scouting missions. I would awake to the sound of gunfire in the distance, and could only hope he was not in trouble. Chabelita was always there, though, to comfort me or distract me with stories about her home village.

Ultimately, Chabelita was badly hurt trying to care for me. We were climbing down a particularly dangerous ledge in the darkness, so she went ahead a few steps to find the best footholds. A stone gave way under her, and she fell to the rocks far below. Watching her, I was sure she had been killed, but we found her alive, with a badly fractured leg. A lot of us were injured, on those dark climbs. The only trails clear of soldiers were the impassable ones.

On the tenth day, though, we staggered into a small village. It was a Mayan community, but you must not tell the name. Can you believe that the entire village came running to help us? There we were, ragged, bloody, armed and in uniform, and they still took us in and cared for us, even though the army was searching for us everywhere. I collapsed completely as we arrived. My legs had kept moving for as long as they had to, but once we reached safety, I had nothing left. A gray-haired, old *campesino* picked me up and carried me into a hut. His wife cleared off the bed for me, and they dressed me in clean clothes and washed my wounded face. Then—I will always remember this—she fixed me a good, strong soup that I could drink through the IV tubes. It was my first real food in so many days. I swear that this soup saved my life. Mario came to the hut, too, and stayed with me until I was taken away to the city.

Everyone was taken in and hidden. For most of our *compas*, hiding was easy. Dressed in civilian clothes, they became the Mayan *campesinos* they had been before the war. No one would know they had not been born there. They rested and helped work in the fields, while the villagers took care of the wounded and brought us food and news about the army activities nearby. The villagers also smuggled messages for us to the capital to help us reconnect with another platoon and to arrange medical care for us. The entire village could have been wiped out for this, but no one ever spoke of us, no one ever gave us away. A community commitment had been made to take care of us, and that commitment was honored by every single villager. Few words were spoken, and they never asked for thanks or payment. To me, it is people like these who are the true heroes of this war. Even though you must not tell the name of this village, you must tell what these people gave to us, what they risked for us.

I think we were there for close to a month while arrangements were made. Mario had made contact with his brother, Alejo, in the capital, and I was to stay with him in one of our safe houses while I received medical treatment. Alejo was the older one, and had brought Mario into the movement. The two brothers were incredibly close. I was happy to think that I would have a chance to know him, but when the car came to take me away, it was very difficult. I knew what Mario was going back to, and that we would probably never see each other again. And in fact we never did. Maybe this part I will not talk about. I arrived safely in the capital, which was no small achievement given my marked face and all the army roadblocks. Alejo took me in and cared for me as his own sister.

I wish this story had a happier ending, but it doesn't. It was early 1982, when the terror in the capital was at its height. The *compas* in our urban front fought bravely to the very end, but they came close to extermination. In the mountains, you stand a chance, but in the city there was just too much surveillance, too many terrified informants trying to get their own family members out of torture cells. We had a number of houses in the capital, but we watched them fall, one by one. Sometimes it was on television, the footage of tanks and bazookas destroying a quiet, middle-class home on a tree-lined street. Sometimes it was in the papers. There were many pictures of the dead, our *compas*, sometimes shot to death, often tortured. We all knew that our time was not far off.

I was being treated in secret clinics since I was not safe in a hospital. With my kind of injury, the authorities would have dragged me away in a matter of hours. But I had received a bone graft, and was healing up at the house with Alejo and the others caring for me. Alejo was very special. It was he who really kept our spirits up during this awful time. A woman named Carmen would come to pick me up every few days, and take me to the clinics for antibiotics and treatment. It was the only time I left the house at all, and I felt very vulnerable, very exposed on these trips. I trusted Carmen completely, though. She was highly intelligent and quick-witted. I think she was from an upper-class family, the way she dressed and spoke, and the way people reacted to her, jumping to obey her smallest requests. With me, though, she was always very genuine and respectful, eager to help and determined to find everything that I needed. After my second month she was captured and tortured to death. This part, also, maybe I will not talk about.

Our house was informed immediately of her capture, and we all sat down to an emergency session. Carmen knew where we were located, so it was a matter of hours before the army would arrive at our front door. We were all weeping, but we knew we had to be clear-minded and make quick arrangements. There were no large safe houses left, we were one of the last ones. We would have to divide up and scatter among the smaller houses of our collaborators. We each received an address, and the *compas* began leaving one by one, a few minutes apart, with the clothes on their back and nothing else. There was only time for a quick embrace and whispered wishes for good luck. I started to leave with Alejo, but our *responsable* decided that we must separate, that our only chance for survival lay in splitting up. So Alejo and I held each other close for a moment and promised that whoever survived would tell Mario how much we had loved him.

I left first, wrapping my face as best I could in a scarf, and pulling up the collar on my jacket. I didn't dare go far in the daylight, so I went into a dimly lit bar, and spent the afternoon there, ordering alcohol I couldn't drink and watching the news on the large television screen. I watched as Carmen's face was shown, elegant in a bouffant hairdo, with news of her tragic death in a terrible car accident. I watched the live footage of our house burning to the ground, collapsed under a rain of bullets and explosives. There was a brief photograph of Alejo's dead and battered face, with word of the capture of yet another terrorist. By then, it had grown dark, and I could watch no more, so I left and found my way to the new address.

This is hard, so hard to tell. Of all the wonderful people in that house, I am the only survivor. The others are all dead, so they cannot help me speak now. But they were all willing to die for our struggle. Their eyes were open. The worst pain, for me, is to think that they may be forgotten someday. Those of us who knew them will never forget. With us they live forever. But outside of Guatemala? Does anyone know how much these people have given to their homeland?

Ruben

The City, ah God, you want me to tell you about the City. But it is such a terrible story, my friend, inspiring, but so terrible. Why do you ask this? Our people were heroic, it is true, but we lost too many of them, far too many. I survived, because my friends were able to smuggle me out to the mountains before I was captured. But the memories, really it is something I still cannot talk about, even though I would like to. There are too many scars—I am truly sorry. You see, already my hands are beginning to tremble just from thinking about it! I am not as strong as some of the others. I have a better idea. I will tell you about my little daughter, Valentina, whom I miss very much. I like to think about her, and it is an easier story for me to remember. But it will also tell you something about what the City was like back then.

I had separated from my wife that year. She was a good woman, very fair-minded and hard-working. We had met as student activists in the university, and for a long time, we had so much in common. But especially after Valentina was born, she began to draw back from our political commitments, to become afraid. Who can blame her? So many of our friends were disappearing. In the end, though, she was afraid to live with me any longer, and she moved into a tiny apartment with the baby. I was hurt, of course, but I stayed with the underground, moving constantly and trying to keep sane. I missed Valentina terribly. She was only two then, and the one real bright spot in my life. Whenever I was living in a safe place for a while, I would bring her home with me for a few hours. I knew there was not much time left for me, at least not in the City, and I wanted to teach her things, to tell her my ideas, while I could. And I wanted her to know that I loved her, that I was still her father, no matter what.

My rules with Valentina were that she could play with anything at all in my apartment except my desk drawer, which was full of papers. If she wanted to dump all my socks out of the dresser to play with, she was allowed to. If she wanted to bang all the pots and pans together, this was also okay with me. The neighbors next door didn't always like it, but really, what harm was she doing? The noise never lasted that long. I didn't even really mind when she got into my papers, because actually, she was always very careful of my things. She just wanted to see what was there. So she would explore everything in sight, and I would talk to her about all my thoughts, as if she were an adult. When I am sad sometimes, I take all of these good memories out, like photographs, and go through them over and over again until I feel better.

The only serious problem I ever had with Valentina was about my pistol. Yes, I had one I kept in the cupboard over the stove, loaded. If the death squads had come after me, I couldn't have stopped them, not with that puny little thing, but I had no intention of being taken alive and tortured. I had decided that if I had to die, I was going to take a few of the torturers with me. That would be my final contribution. What I hadn't counted on, of course, was Valentina. It never occurred to me that she could climb up to that cabinet. She was still so little. But I can tell you that you should never, never underestimate a two-year-old. I came back from the grocery store at the corner one day and found her dragging my pistol, with great resolve on her little face, into the back yard. And she was really very irate with me for taking it away. After all, she had captured it fair and square.

I was very frightened for a long time after that. What if the neighbors had seen this? Guns are illegal for all but the army and the government people in Guatemala. For me to be caught with a pistol back then meant immediate arrest as a subversive. In other words, death. There were no such things as trials for the politically suspect. Worse yet, what if I had not come back so quickly, and Valentina had accidentally shot herself with the bullets I was keeping for myself? These thoughts made me frantic. I tried to talk to her about this, but the more I explained, the more curious she became, and more than once I found her on her way to the forbidden cabinet. Finally, I decided that I had to take desperate measures.

One day I packed up Valentina and also my pistol and we went away to a place that I cannot tell you about. It was not far from the City, and it was where I had first learned to fire a gun. I carried Valentina out to the target range and explained to her one more time that guns were very bad things, that they could kill people, and that they must be stayed away from. Then I picked her up and cuddled her in my left arm, so that she would not be too frightened, and took the pistol in my right hand. I fired three shots—one, two, three—into the target, looking Valentina in the eye between each shot.

How I hated to teach her this, my own child. I had forgotten how strong the kick on those things was and how loud the sound. With each shot, I hissed the word "fuck!" to myself. "Fuck, fuck, fuck!" just to let out all of my own tensions. Valentina did not like any of this, and nodded in agreement when I said that really, guns were things to be left alone. And from that day on she never did go near the cabinet over the stove again.

I had pretty much forgotten about the whole thing, when several months later I was taking her back to her mother's house. We had to cross the main square, near the National Palace, to catch the right bus. I never much liked that place, so full of soldiers and police, but it was late and we were hurrying. I was holding her up close to me, waiting in line for the bus, when she reached up quietly and tugged at my beard. "Papa", she said to me in a very intent little voice. "Papa." I asked her what was wrong, but she wouldn't answer. Instead, she moved her little eyes all the way to the left, as if to point, but without using her finger. She pulled my face down close to hers, then, and whispered, "Papa, Papa! Fuck, fuck, fuck!" And when I looked in the direction that she had moved her eyes, sure enough, there was a burly man standing nearby, a large handgun protruding from under his vest. I don't know who he was, but he was clearly trouble. Valentina had been trying to warn me, and somehow, from the way she was growing up there in the City during that terrible time, she had known not to point or say the words even. Her mother and I had not taught her these things. She just knew. She had been watching us.

Well, my little Valentina must be nearly twelve now. It is hard for me to believe. But when this is over, I know what I want more than anything to do, and that is to go and see her. I want to take her in my arms and talk with her for hours, and catch up on all the times we have missed with each other. I want to hear all of her stories and to tell her all of mine. And this one, the one I have just told you, will be the very first I will share with her.

Fernando

I can see from your face that you do not like weapons. Here, let me move my rifle out of the way for you. I want you to be comfortable while we are talking. Take my jacket, too, for a cushion. Is that better?

Guns, guns, they are everywhere up here—we sleep with them at our sides; we bring them to the riverside when we bathe. This must seem very strange to you, but you do not know what it was like when we did not have enough weapons to defend ourselves with. I have been up here in the mountains for eleven years. In the beginning I didn't like weapons that much either, since I had once been a student of theology. But our lives without enough weapons I liked even less. I will tell you a story about guns. Maybe you will understand, maybe you won't.

Years ago I was sent out on a scouting mission with two other *compañeros*. Their names were Guillermo and Tino. I want you to remember their names, because they were good people, very sincere and straightforward. Tino was like an older brother to me, always teaching me new things. Guillermo was my own age, and like me, eager and very idealistic. They are both dead now, which is why I ask you to remember their names. They died because they were willing to risk their lives fighting in a poor people's army.

The soldiers had been bombing our base area very heavily, and we needed to move to a safer location. That was our assignment, to find the safer

119

location. We had spent more than a week edging through the trees and lying still in the heavy brush while the soldiers marched past us. We made note of the enemy positions and the directions of their movements, counted their platoons and found their helicopter landing areas. It was a dangerous assignment, but by the end of the week we had found a remote but beautiful spot very high up on the volcano. From there we would have a natural lookout over the entire valley below us. The three of us were so happy to find this place, after such a difficult week, that we decided to stop and rest there for a little while. There was a spring of cold water nearby, so we took turns bathing while the others kept watch, then sat down together for a brief meal. As we ate, I looked down below us. It was the springtime then, and all was green, and we were so high up that I could watch the mists below us, rising up the slopes. For a few moments, I felt at peace. You are a foreigner and have seen many different places, but tell me, do you not find our country to be very beautiful?

The peaceful moment did not last for long. As we were gathering up our packs, shots rang out, and a bullet hit the rock that I was sitting on. The soldiers had somehow found our trail, and followed us to this place. We grabbed our rifles and threw ourselves to the ground, crawling into the dense green foliage nearby. The soldiers were close by. I could hear them laughing and shouting insults at us, telling us that our time had come to die. Tino tricked them, though, leading us down a tiny trail he had noticed on the way up. We were able to escape into a wooded area and break into a run down the steep slopes, hoping the head start Tino had given us would be enough. Perhaps if we had been closer to our base camp, we would have made it, or if we had had more ammunition. But we had already been through two brief skirmishes that week, and our supplies were very low.

We ran for a very long time. It was a dead run, a run for our lives, the soldiers never very far behind us. We would try to run straight through the trees, using them as cover, allowing the heavy branches to slash at our faces, and every so often one of us would get down and return fire, driving the enemy back, winning us a few moments of time. It was not long, though, before we were down to our last thirty bullets. We could only look at each other then, because there was nothing to be said.

I am the survivor of that day. Guillermo went down first, shot through the head as he tried to cover us. Tino grabbed Guillermo's bullet pouch and kept running with me. I took the next shot, here, through the left arm, you can still see the scar. But I was young, and I wanted so badly to live that it didn't slow me down much. It was Tino who took the bad wound, through the thigh, stopping him from running. I grabbed him by the arms and dragged him to cover, but as I fumbled at his leg, he shot himself through the head to force me to leave him. So I took his bullets, and Guillermo's, and kept running, too out of breath to weep.

At times like that, so many things flash through your mind. Your life, the *compas*, your family, everything slides wildly by, in a big jumble. But I will tell you one feeling that I will never forget, and that is the rage. If we had only had more bullets, we could have driven the soldiers back and bought ourselves the time we needed to escape. Everyone always accuses us of being puppets of Moscow, or Cuba, of not being a real grassroots revolution, even though the majority of us are Mayan. We were in Guatemala before the Europeans. Yet there we were that day, dying in our own homeland, because we were down to thirty bullets. If we were really puppets, don't you think we would have been better armed and equipped? We were being hunted because we supposedly are foreign invaders, but we were dying because we are not. The irony of it—it still gives me rage.

Amelia

Have a peanut butter cracker? No? Yeah, well, it is a little stale, I know. But look, food like this don't come so easy up here in the mountains. It's like the saying goes, when there is there is, when there's not, there's not. So come on, eat up. Also, peanut butter has protein in it, and that's good for you. Besides, some villagers gave me these on the last campaign, so we should especially appreciate them. They are signs of affection from the people. And courage. It's dangerous for them to give us anything at all. I can remember when it wasn't so easy. I'll tell you a story about popular support that I bet will make you eat those crackers.

This happened maybe ten years ago, not long after I came up into the mountains. I was about seventeen, I would guess. It was back when I didn't know the terrain very well. I got lost a lot, only back then it wasn't so funny. Lost meant dead. It was also back when we didn't have enough guns to defend ourselves with. Weapons were so precious, and I had just been issued my rifle. I remember all this, because it became so important later on.

We were camped out in a coffee orchard, and rations had been very tight that week. We had walked and walked, and I had gone to bed hungry, and with no idea where we were. This didn't really worry me, because I trusted the others to know our location. This was a mistake. Up here, you must always know where you are. You must always be ready to survive on your own.

My hunger made me wake up early that morning, so I crept towards the small spring of water near our camp, to drink and to wash my face. Ernesto was there too, drinking and looking happy. "Amelia," he told me, "come with me quick. I've found a little tree here with four big ripe avocados." He grabbed me by the arm, and pulled me a few trees away to show me. Ernesto always shared everything with me. And sure enough, there were four perfect avocados there for us, just waiting to be eaten, and we gobbled them down as quick as you can imagine. They were delicious, and we were both really very hungry, which made them taste even better.

It was while we were sitting there so contentedly that the first explosions hit us. There was shrapnel flying everywhere, and smoke, and the "rat-a-tat" of machine gun fire. I threw myself on the ground and started crawling towards an irrigation canal I had seen, thinking it would be the best escape route out of the orchard. There were two other *compañeras* there, cat-crawling down the side of the ditch, but even as I watched, they came under a rain of bullets, and one fell, shot through the small of her back. So I fled back into the orchard, running zig-zag through the trees, until I was out of the range of fire. There I found Ernesto, sitting dazed on the ground, a bullet hole drilled neatly through the folds of his throat. He was alive but bleeding heavily. Neither one of us knew where we were, and we certainly couldn't call out to the other *compañeros*. Just as we were hunting for our friends, so the army would be hunting for us, hoping to catch stragglers like ourselves. I bandaged up Ernesto as best I could and hauled him to his feet, and together we began cautiously combing the orchard, square by square. We kept this up for a long time, but it was a big orchard, and we could find no one at all. We could only hear sporadic bursts of the machine gun fire, here and there throughout the orchard. The air reeked of ripening coffee beans and smoke. Ernesto needed water and medical help. I don't know how he kept walking, even with me supporting him, but he did. I guess he knew he had to.

We eventually came to the edge of the orchard and a small road that led to a village. We headed that way to look for water and directions back to our platoon. I felt very confident then; the villagers had always helped me before. They would care for Ernesto and show me the back trails. It never occurred to me that we could be turned away. As we neared the houses we came upon a small cluster of women, who stared at us in fear. You can imagine why. Our uniforms were covered with Ernesto's blood, and I was carrying both rifles over one arm. There was gunfire in the distance, and the women shrank back, listening. I told them not to be afraid, that we were the *compañeros*, and that we would never hurt them. I told them that Ernesto was badly injured. Would they give us some water, and help get him bandaged up? One of the women started forward with her water jug, but another one, maybe her mother, stopped her, terror on her face. We could hear the sound of new explosions coming from the orchard. The other women looked down at their feet, motionless. Well, this made me really angry, you can be sure. Here was Ernesto, bleeding his life away for these people, all for them, so their lives would be better, without so much suffering, and they were too afraid to give him water. I told them this, and asked them, how could they deny him water, when he was dying for them? But the women only looked away. Finally the younger one pointed towards the orchard. The army would kill them, she explained simply.

And so I had to move on, dragging Ernesto. He was beginning to loose consciousness, but would wake up, here and there, and tell me to leave him, to run. And even though I'm really strong, I was growing more and more tired. I found other people, but they all turned away in fear, just like the first ones. I crept around the entire perimeter of the village this way, begging for help, hiding behind the trees, growing very desperate, crying because I was sure Ernesto was going to die, surrounded by his own terrified people, without the help he needed. This was very bitter for me. I have never forgotten.

Finally, I saw a small house off to the side of the trail, behind some trees, a good distance from the village. Because it was hard to see the house, I hoped the people there would have more courage. And anyway, it was my last hope. I dragged Ernesto through the bushes right up to the door, which I kicked open. A family was inside sitting around a small wooden table, and they leaped up when we came falling across the threshold. They were good people, too, frightened, of course, but they helped us. The woman ran to clear a bed for Ernesto, and bring fresh water, while her daughter, silent, tore a clean cloth into bandages. I spoke quietly with the father for awhile, and he agreed to hide Ernesto for one day while I found our platoon. He would dress him in civilian clothes. But even so, after one day it would no longer be safe. The army was everywhere, like angry hornets, he explained. And so I got some instructions from him, and drank some water, and left, even though I was exhausted

It was dark out, no moon or stars that night, but I was still able to find the beginning of the trail he had told me about. It would lead to a small town about fifteen miles away, where I knew I could find help. A *compañero* had taken me through there, months earlier, and pointed to a house where two elderly people lived. They were *compañeros* also, he told me. In case of emergency, I could always go there, and they would know what to do. So I took off at a fast pace, hopeful. At first the darkness made me feel safer, and I found myself hurrying even faster to reach the town before dawn, when once again I would become visible to the enemy. And so I walked and walked, for hours and hours, but in the end I missed a turn-off somehow and became hopelessly lost. I only gave up when I came to the edge of what seemed to be a huge pit; my foot reached the edge and found no bottom. I tossed a pebble into the darkness and could not hear it land. Try as I would, I could see nothing, so finally I sat down under a small tree and cried myself to sleep.

At dawn, a gentle hand shook me awake, and I started to my feet, disoriented. A young *campesino*, about my own age, stood before me, eyeing my blood-caked uniform. He touched my face lightly, eyes full of concern, and began brushing the dirt and leaves off my clothes. He called me his little sister, and asked if I were hungry. It was only later that he told me that when he first saw me, he had thought I was dead, and had approached to bury me. Without asking me any questions, he brought out a small canteen of water, a mango, and some corn tortillas, which I wolfed down. Then he told me that the army was nearby, that I would have to get out of my uniform quickly, before I was seen. I should wait there for him; he would return home and bring a dress of his sister's and some shoes. Then we would talk about my needs. And I trusted him. Our training teaches us to trust no one, and this is right, of course. But I had very little choice. And do you know, my instincts just told me that it was all right, that he would not betray me. And my instincts were right. His name was Raoul, and he saved my life.

Raoul came back and gave me the clothes, then helped me dig a small hole under the tree to bury my rifle and my uniform in. He helped me get my bearings, so that later I would be able to come back and retrieve it. Then he took my hand and started walking me to the village I was trying to reach. It was more than ten miles away still—I was way off course—so this time he was going to guide me. If anyone stopped us, I was to say I was his cousin, from the Santos family, and that I was going to visit my relatives. And so off we went, across the corn fields and through the forests. I remember little about the terrain or the people we passed, I just remember the strangeness of wearing a dress again, my fears for Ernesto, and my enormous gratitude to Raoul. We spoke quietly as we walked. He asked me about the war, why I had decided to fight, where I was from. He was surprised to hear that I had finished high school, that I could have had a comfortable life back in the city, if I had so chosen. He told me that it was he who should be grateful to me, and to all the others like me who were fighting for the rest of them, to make their lives better. When I told him about the women the day before, in the village, he cried.

We reached the town in the early afternoon but waited, hidden in the trees, for darkness to return, so that we would not be seen entering the house. I grew very anxious then, sitting still with nothing to do. What if the old couple were no longer there? What if they were dead? What if they could not help me? What if I couldn't find the house? What if Ernesto had died during the night? A day had already passed. I had not been able to keep my promise to return within twenty-four hours. Had the army found the place where I had left him?

In the end, though, Raoul and I did find the house. I recognized the fountain with the little dog sculpture on it, because it had reminded me before of the puppy I had left behind, at home. And as I stumbled through the door, I knew that we were saved, because the most wonderful old people in the world were there to help us. They threw their arms around us both and pulled us into the house, then ran for food and water. The old lady wrapped my swollen feet in hot towels, and massaged my aching arms, calling me her dearest daughter. They heaped food on Raoul's plate, more and more, reminding him that their house was his own. We told them about Ernesto, about my platoon, and the old man disappeared for a bit, then came back smiling, telling us that all was well, all was arranged. I fell asleep then, in a soft bed, lulled as the woman combed my long hair smooth across the pillows. When I awoke late the next morning, Raoul was already gone, without even giving me a chance to thank him.

And so I did get back to my platoon after another two days of climbing into the mountains. But it was easy to climb now, because I was so relieved to be going home again. And would you believe that when I got back, Ernesto was sitting there at the fire, waiting for me? Weak as he was, he jumped up when he saw me and swung me right off my feet in a great big hug. I would have started crying again, but he smiled impishly at me and asked me, in a croaking voice, if I would like to eat a few avocados—he knew just the tree.

But the rest of the story did not end so happily. My rifle was still down in the valley, buried under the tree where Raoul and I had left it, and after I had rested for a few days, the *comandante* sent me back down, with two other *compas*, to go and find it. Rifles could not be spared back then; it was not possible. So off the three of us went together. I was not afraid this time, because the others with me knew the terrain so perfectly. It was only when we reached the tree that my heart sank. The small pit was open, and the rifle was gone. A villager was gathering firewood, not far away, and when we asked for the news he told us that the army had been there the day before, with Raoul. They had shot him that night, and left his battered body on his mother's doorstep. She was weeping still. It was the same at the other village. The old couple was gone, dragged from their beds in the middle of the night and never seen again. Their little house had been burned to the ground. Nothing remained but the small fountain with the carved puppy.

And so these three people had died for me. They knew the risks, and helped me anyway, because they believed in what we are doing up here, because they knew that we were fighting for them. I am sad, very sad, when I remember them, but the pain has made me strong. It is because of them that I am still here. If these wonderful people could die for me, then I can certainly fight it out until the triumph or until my death. Whatever it takes, I'm ready.

Camilo
Talks About Food

Food is very dear to our hearts. This you can understand, I am sure. Most of us grew up hungry, and our diet here, although sufficient, is not luxurious. There is coffee, rice, corn, beans, *atole*, and wild roots and herbs. We do not go hungry, not any more. But we all love to think about meats and breads and chocolates and cigarettes. Me, I like to think of a spicy sausage I ate at a carnival many years ago. So much flavor, I can taste it still. There was a thick, rolled-up pancake, too, with a sweet sauce. That was the night before I left for the mountains so long ago. I had spent the evening walking all over my small town, taking one last look. It is not so much the town I miss now, for my true friends and family are here with me. But the food, ah, that is another story. We are all the same about these things. Did you know that when we fall in love, we exchange spoons with our sweethearts as a sign of our affection?

It is the people from your part of the world, from North America, that I just cannot understand, not when it comes to food, anyway. Don't you like good flavors, well-prepared meals? You can have anything to eat that you want, and yet your foods, at least the ones I have tried, are so terrible. Please don't be offended, my friend. It is just that I don't understand, and here you are sitting right next to me to tell me all about it.

I have never been to your country, of course, so

Life in the Revolution

I am hardly an expert on this subject. But I will tell you about my one experience with American food that has left me wondering all these years. This happened close to this very volcano, as a matter of fact. There was a large plantation, owned by a very wealthy family, a very right-wing family, as well, I might add. They were very firmly on the side of the military, even during the times of the massacres, which I find hard to understand. It was not their beliefs, however, which drew our attention to them. It was their actions. They were allowing their lands to be used as a military base, and turning our people in to the authorities to be picked up and tortured. This, of course, we could not allow. We contacted them several times about these activities, warning them that they should limit their conduct to civilian affairs if they wished to be treated as civilians. They would be treated as a military target if they behaved as such. Of course, they did not take us seriously at all. Few people did back then. So after some time passed without any change on their part, we decided that we would have to take action.

We watched the place for a long time, waiting until most of the soldiers were away on a special excursion. Then we came down very late at night for a surprise raid. The few soldiers who had stayed behind simply ran off after the first few minutes of battle. I don't think their morale was very high, and there were no officers present to order them to hold their ground. So after only a brief skirmish, we were able to stroll right onto the property unimpeded. It was harvest time, and the sheds were brimming with cotton, which we quietly set afire. In this way the workers would not suffer hunger, only the owner would lose his profits. The bright flames billowed high into the air, but no one from the big house came out to speak with us. So we walked up to the front door and called for someone to come outside and talk. We wanted to talk to them, tell them why we had burned their cotton, and tell them what changes we expected from them.

But the family had run off with the soldiers, fearing that we had come to kill them. The house stood empty but for an elderly Mayan servant, who opened the door for us. She listened quietly as we explained why we had come, and why we had taken action against the plantation. She nodded as we spoke, and suddenly, our evening's work was completed. "Mission accomplished," as they say in your movies, right? We had expected a much more difficult night. So, after talking for a few minutes, we decided that we might as well go into the kitchen and make ourselves a meal. We were all pretty hungry and there was bound to be plenty of food on a big plantation like that. Good food, too, we assumed. After all, this was a kitchen of the rich.

In the pantry we found all kinds of fancy, shining cans and jars of food, many with labels in languages we couldn't understand. We understood the pictures, though, and just for fun, we decided to try the imported stuff first, since it would be new and different. That was where the fun ended. We tried some of your breakfast cereals—I think it was Cheerios—then had some cold meat from a can. These were a big disappointment, so we tried some canned string beans and carrots, and these were even worse. Finally, we went on to powdered milk and instant potatoes and instant frijoles from little paper sacks. I will never forget the powdered frijoles. These were truly dreadful, my friend. How can anyone ruin plain beans? And the orange powder that was supposed to turn into orange juice? What on earth was that? After a little while, we became very full, but very frustrated, and decided to go on home. In the future, we would stick to the good food the villagers passed to us.

We talked about this food for a long time. Yankee food, as we had seen it, became almost legendary for a while. We just couldn't understand it. Why would anyone want fast food that was so fast you couldn't tell the beans from the potatoes without looking at the labels? Why would anyone want something as nice as food to be fast? Me, I like to sit over my meals for as long as possible, and enjoy every bite. We tried to imagine how people in your country must live, and for a long time we joked that the *gringos* were so good at taking all the fun out of life that they had probably even learned how to have babies, sex free, out of tin cans.

The City,
as Remembered
by Jennifer

When I left for Guatemala I thought I was taking a one-month trip. My plans were so neat, so tidy, so professional. I would travel first to the capital, carrying courteous letters of introduction for certain persons there, then move into the countryside a bit to speak with church people and civic leaders. My objective was to gather current and credible information on the areas our clients were from, so that we could support their asylum claims with concrete data. I would return with well-organized and detailed files and testify myself. If the courts wouldn't believe our clients, on the grounds that they were just trying to win citizenship in our wealthy country, well then, they would have to believe me. I was born in the U.S.A. (even if my grandparents weren't), so they would have to listen to me.

But things were never so simple. I did not get out after one month, or two, or even six, or even a year. I ended up with a tiny apartment, filled with books and tapes in a padlocked trunk, two pairs of boots—one for rocks and one for jungle mud—and one or two battered Guatemalans, if not hidden under the bed, at least off the streets until safe passage to another country could be arranged. The military, out of money after ravaging the country with its mad counterinsurgency campaign, was once again courting the United States for military aid. Until this delicate matter could be resolved in a gentlemanly fashion, atrocities could not be committed against or in the presence of any North Americans. The Yankee embassy was not to be disturbed.

It was in this way that I forgot about immigration and began a new career, as a diminutive body guard of sorts. If I slept at the home of a friend, the hated telephone would most likely not ring that night, nor any cars arrive to drag the person away to the limbo of the "disappeared." I listened and listened to the numbing stories of my hosts and wondered how they had survived, how they had stayed sane. Once, after hearing a mother tell me of her lost son, I awoke in the middle of the night to find her standing in the shadows, sobbing, as she ironed and re-ironed his fading shirts.

Not everyone did survive. It was early on that a pretty young mother vanished before she reached the airport, where her escape route to safety awaited her. All arrangements had been made, but she disappeared somewhere between her home and the ticket counter. They found her soon enough, naked and battered, hands hacked off, face destroyed. Sickened, I thought about leaving Guatemala then, but was too busy to do anything about it. There was too much to do.

The city was surreal. On the surface all was quiet, all was peaceful. It was so easy to be a tourist, walk to the markets, enjoy the foods, buy the beautiful weavings from the quaint Indian people. Certainly no one was going to risk their necks talking to foreigners about what was really happening. It was only with time that you could see: the young student running for his life across the square, the unionist's three-year-old son struck down by bullets aimed at his father, the cars with darkened windows parked just at the corner, waiting.

After the first few months, I had an image of a city with a decimated population, a crowd of people with great holes where the writers and unionists and civic leaders had once been but were no more. Perhaps they were dead, perhaps disappeared, perhaps driven into exile in fear of their lives. As time passed, and I learned more, this image changed. I began to see a vast and devastated field of ashes, with only the stunned survivors wandering about, trying to pull the pieces of their smashed society from the wreckage. Like many Guatemalans, I learned that it was better not to think about these things, to take one day at a time, to concentrate on living. I began to take a teenaged girl from a destroyed clan to a dance hall every Saturday night, to teach her to dance, and to fight off depression with the wild salsa rhythms. We became much sought after dance partners, learning not only to forget but to enjoy, the true key to remaining sane. I bought my first pair of red shoes.

Time passed, and I became more confident, more resilient. Even so, there were times when I found myself struck down by some new tragedy, even though it was no worse than all the others. All my hard won defenses would crumble, and I would find myself weeping for hours in a darkened room. It was that way with Rosario, a young woman with a baby. Her husband, a leader of the University Student Association, had been kidnapped during a sweep of the campus, and had never returned home. Heartbroken, she helped to organize the GAM, a mutual support group for relatives of the disappeared. I never met her, but saw her photographs often, a slender woman with much dignity and a sweet face, marching side by side with barefooted Mayan widows in the city square. She was everywhere, speaking to the public, giving interviews, writing pamphlets, and petitioning the government. She seemed tireless. From a distance, it seemed clear how much she had loved her husband and how desperate she was to get him back. The months passed, and she must have known that she would never see him again. In her pictures she became thinner and sadder, and I grieved for her. I thought, once, of sending her flowers, but never had the chance.

It was during Easter week that she died—she, her younger brother, and her two-year-old son. A few days earlier another founder of the GAM had been dragged away in front of witnesses. He was found dead the next day, killed with a blow torch. Rosario spoke movingly at his funeral, then returned home to care for her feverish baby. Frightened by the constant death threats against her, she dared not leave the house for several days, but finally ventured forth to a nearby pharmacy in search of medicine for her child. She took the little boy with her, and her nineteen-year-old brother, for protection. They never returned home. After many hours of despair by her friends and family, her car was found far outside the City, the three pitiful bodies slumped across the seats. The authorities announced a tragic car crash, the cause of death, broken necks. Rosario's mother, clutching the arm of her only surviving son, agreed publicly with the official report. Relations with the U.S. Embassy continued undisturbed.

It was a long time before anyone would talk about what had really happened. But in the end, people began to speak clandestinely, choked with sobs and gagged by terror, of the evidence of torture such as the bite marks they had seen on Rosario's breasts at the morgue. In a darkened church basement, an elderly friend of the family told of the funeral, of what she knew. She spoke of the religious convictions of the family, how Rosario and her brother had been laid out in their coffins with their arms crossed, like good Catholics. Yet the child's arms had lain straight at his sides, the palms of his hands facing upwards. Already furious over the murders, the friend went from relative to relative in the room, demanding an explanation, but meeting only terrified eyes. Finally, the friend was told to stop asking questions and look at the child's fingers. She returned to the coffin, hesitated, then turned over one tiny dead hand. Where the thumbnail should have been, there was only a small crust of blood. She could look no further, and quickly turned the hand back over. Raising her head, she caught the eyes of Rosario's mother, watching her from the other side of the room, beseeching her without words to press no further. The surviving brother sat nearby.

I took to my room for a long while after that. I packed and unpacked my bags, tried to think of other people who still lived, tried to go back to the dance hall, but couldn't for awhile. Rosario's face haunted me so. Her photograph was everywhere, defiantly posted on street corners and buildings across the city, and she looked out at us all with those large, dark eyes, and that soft, sad mouth. The worst was knowing that I could do nothing. She was already dead, had already witnessed the torture and murder of her own child. And the military was still in power, thanks largely to the use of my own tax dollars. I stayed in my room.

Finally, an old friend came to visit, bringing his little boy with him. This friend was from the highlands, and had fought for many years with the guerrillas in the mountains. In the end he was badly wounded, though, and had been forced to move down into the city with his *compañera*. There his son, the apple of his eye, was born. We talked for a long time that afternoon, about the Maya, about Guatemala, about Rosario, about life. He was so calm and tranquil, picking up crayons, answering his little son's endless question, comforting me. I asked him how he had survived so many terrible years, how he had kept his humanity through times of such inhumanity. He spoke of perspective then, and of patience, the need to see things in the big framework. Speaking for himself, he had survived many combats. He had participated fully in something he so passionately believed in. He had lived to see the birth of his son, and the turning point in the war. So many of his friends had died without seeing any of this. The triumph back then had only been a distant dream. He considered himself a most fortunate man. Even if he could not survive to see the end, he already felt fulfilled. He and the others like him had served as a bridge, the bridge from a terrible past to a future where these things could never happen again.

He did not, of course, survive to see the triumph. A few weeks later, I heard that he had been dragged from his office building by a group of heavily-armed men. They had forced him into a car with military plates and black glass windows, and he was never seen again. I heard from the witnesses that he put up a good fight, though. The men couldn't get him into the car until they had broken both of his legs.

After that I went back to my room, but not to cry any more. Instead, I packed a lightweight duffel bag and strapped a pair of mud boots to one end. I cleaned up my room and sent my notes and tapes out of the country with a friend. Then I walked downtown and caught a bus headed for a remote jungle area. It was time to see what else was happening in this mad and cruel land.

Why and How

You ask me why and how these things can happen. The why of it, only God can answer, my child. I wish I knew myself, so that I could give more comfort to those who come to me. But I can only join them in prayer, for I have no explanations. The how of it all, I can tell you in part, for part of it I have seen for myself. You remember the young man I spoke to you about before? I had thought to try and help him leave the country. But there is no need now. He has gone quite insane, and is in danger no longer. He lives there in the church with us, and we care for him as best we can. You see, he was once a soldier.

No, no, you must not look at me with such surprise. The Church will always shelter those who seek to repent, and this young man is not at fault. Let me tell you his story and see if you don't agree with me, and even feel sorry for him. Life has treated him cruelly enough.

This soldier, or rather, this deserter, is quite young. He was even younger when he enlisted, although enlisted is a euphemism. He grew up in a remote Mayan village and could neither read nor write, nor even speak much Spanish, when the army came to town. There was no formal registration of anyone. The military truck simply pulled up on the football field, and the soldiers took all the young men away, including him. He had just turned fifteen years of age a short while earlier, but no one asked about that. There was not even time to say farewell to his family. When the truck stopped, he was at the army base.

Basic training was very difficult for him. He and his friends were jeered at and beaten until they learned to communicate in Spanish. The Mayan languages were not allowed. The work load was heavy, although this did not disturb him as much as the constant humiliations and cruelty. He had grown up with a heavy work load, but also with pride in his people and his heritage. At the base, this was taken away, day by day. He also hated the political training, to hear the disrespect given his people, to hear that in the mountains, the guerrillas were all communists and Cubans and Soviets. He had seen the *compañeros* near his village before, and knew they were of his own people and no other. The soldiers told him that the guerrillas were committing atrocities, yet he knew who had killed his older brother. He heard these things and had his own ideas, but kept them to himself. He learned to survive by accepting, or by seeming to accept. And he trusted no one.

And so his training period passed without disaster. Disaster occurred later, out in the field. Combat had not frightened the young man, although he found it meaningless and sad. But it was after the combat that his commanding officer, angered by the results of the battle, decided to descend on a nearby village. After going house to house for a short time, he returned, dragging a terrified young man with him. Together, they all marched out of the town, and higher up into the mountains, to a place far away from any other people. There, the poor prisoner was given a terrible beating, the officer screaming to him that he was a communist, and must reveal the names of his comrades. To our young man, it was clear that the boy knew nothing, that indeed, he could barely understand the Spanish in which he was being addressed. It was tempting to intercede, to speak up, at least to translate the questions being delivered with such heavy blows. But basic training had taught him to keep silent, to stand back.

When the youth fainted from the beating without answering the questions, the officer seated him in front of a tree, pulling his legs out straight before him, binding his arms around the trunk so tightly that the ropes dug into the flesh. Then he ordered the boy's boots removed, and a fire built. The soldiers were ordered to seize a flaming branch each and to form a line. One by one, they were to take turns burning the boy's feet until he identified his comrades. My young friend was halfway down the line, and sickened as the air filled with the smell of burnt flesh, and the other boy's screams. He said, when he arrived here, that it was like listening to his own screams. When he came to the head of the line he told his officer that he could not burn the other one's feet. He was told to sit down with the prisoner and take off his own boots. He hesitated for a moment, looking at the prisoner, and weighing the burning stick in his hand. Then he burned the boy's raw feet, and listened to his scream—their mutual scream.

After that he simply waited for his chance. It took awhile, but during the next battle he was able to fake his own death on the field, and rejoice as the other soldiers retreated without stopping to recover his body. Then he waited for darkness and tore off his uniform, wandering to a nearby village to beg for help. Help he received, for the others, looking at him, thought of their own children taken away to be soldiers. And finally he arrived here, begging for sanctuary.

I have sheltered and cared for him as well as I can, but with time, he came to lose his mind completely. Now he does not know who he is or where he comes from. He screams out at night, but during the day can only stare out of the windows, muttering. He has found a safe place at last, out there where he is now.

They say that killing comes easier after the first time. That is how the army operates here. The first time is forced, then perhaps, too, the second or third. After that there is no resistance, no shock, and the men simply do as they are told. They no longer feel. Our young man escaped this fate. He lost everything but his conscience. For this I shall always respect him.

Domingo

Look, even if you wanted to hang on to your male ego up here in the mountains, it just isn't possible. I'm telling you it can't be done. I ought to know, because I tried hard enough myself in the beginning. I came up here years ago with some of my school friends, all men friends of course, and we considered ourselves to be pretty hot stuff, very revolutionary and very sexy. We had read all the correct political books that our government had so long censored. We tried our very best to look a bit like Che. Of course it never occurred to us to quit smoking before we went trotting up the slopes of the volcano, so we arrived pretty tired out. But this we attributed to mere changes in altitude. Hey, no problem, right?

It took us a little while to get the hang of cooking and washing and sewing for ourselves. But this we had been expecting, and this we knew was correct. After all, we knew that feminism was a revolutionary concept, and to be respected. So we were cheerful enough about scorching our rice and sewing our buttons on crooked, just as we were cheerful about our sore muscles and blistered feet. All this was as we had envisioned it, and we threw ourselves into our new lives body and soul. We were really very happy. It was the subtler issues that threw us for a loop.

Our first real hurdle was to get over our own dogmatism and to start thinking for ourselves, as Guatemalan *compañeros*. We had grown so used to simply repeating what we read in books. After all,

147

before we arrived in the mountains, the revolution for us was only a dream. The repression and terror down in the city had always been real enough, but this was our first actual experience in the movement. And so it took a while, quite a while in fact, to get used to saying what we thought, instead of what we thought we were supposed to think. Quite often, we didn't even know exactly what we thought, because we'd never done any real analysis or evaluation of our own situation. And so we found ourselves doing a great deal of listening. And this brought us to yet a second hurdle. We found ourselves listening more and more to young Mayan *compañeros* who had a great deal to say. We were not outright racists, for the injustice against Mayan peoples was something none of us could ignore. It was a jolt, though, to realize that these young *campesinos*, who had never had the privilege of attending school, could think circles around us. They would express themselves so simply, and yet their ideas were so profound, so rational. When they finished, there was really nothing for us to add. All this, of course, was part of our growing process, but I can tell you that our egos were taking quite a bruising.

With women it was still another hurdle. Like I said, it was not that we expected them to cook or wash for us. We weren't that backwards. But all the same, we were so very conscious of them being female, a different species really. We wanted to hover over them, help them out, protect them. In other words, to treat them as the weaker sex. The problem was, they didn't need us. It was a sad day for us when we found that we couldn't do as many sit ups as Annabella, or climb as fast as Marisa. But then again, it was easy to blame everything on the altitude, at least in the beginning. And meanwhile, we flirted up a storm with every woman in sight. This was our way of still feeling like real men. And the *compañeras* understood and amiably flirted back, as if we were their favorite younger brothers.

After a few weeks, we all had a terrific crush on the same girl. She was young, maybe sixteen or seventeen, and very pretty, of course. She was Mayan, very slender and lithe, with long, glossy black braids. Her eyes were huge and dark and tilted up, and on each side of her lips she had a deep, sparkly dimple. Her name was Teresa, and remembering her now, I realize what an exceptional *compañera* she was, how hard-working, how decent in her ways, how committed. But we didn't see all this in her back then. We only saw someone young and pretty who would put up with our flirtations and give us the warm smile we so badly needed. We were all madly in love with her at the same time.

It was not long before we encountered our first battle. We had all wanted to get into combat as quickly as possible, in part to work through our unadmitted fears, and in part, so that we would no longer be such complete newcomers. We craved to be experienced and settled in like the others. And quickly enough, the opportunity arrived. We were changing camps, all marching down the slopes towards our new location, when shooting broke out up ahead of us. We had come across an unexpected army patrol and within seconds, the air was full of bullets, smoke and frightening explosions. The noise was something I had never expected, something I was simply not ready for, and for a moment, it stopped me dead in my tracks, together with one of my friends. We were just standing there, rooted to the ground, staring, forgetting everything we had been trained to do. And then suddenly Teresa was running towards us from the rear of our platoon, her rifle lowered and her braids flying. How swift footed she was on that rocky terrain, and how serene she looked! As she rushed past, she grabbed me firmly by one arm, pulling me forwards with her, shoving my rifle into the correct position. She was smiling her encouragement to us all.

"Come on, *compañeros*!" she shrieked over the din. "Don't be frightened, we're all going to stick together now!". And sure enough, her presence somehow gave us courage, and we ran with her to the front of the battle, throwing ourselves to the ground, copying her moves. We kept our heads down like she did and tried to make every bullet count, like she did. She was screaming like a banshee and completely fearless. And before long it was over, and she was hugging us, and the others too, and we realized that we had just survived our very first combat. We also realized that we would never again see women in the same way as we had before.

And so that's how it is up here. You can hang on to your male ego just as hard as you are able, but it's not going to last very long. And this is a good thing, not a bad thing. Because in the end, you discover a new way of relating to women that you never had before. Yes, of course, we still flirt, because after all, what's the fun in life if there isn't any flirtation? Me, for example, I still flirt like crazy whenever I get the chance. But it is so different now.

Because the woman is a real person, someone to share with, not just a pretty little flower to carry around. I never had real relationships with women before. Infatuations, yes, but real relations, understanding, friendships—no. And to think I never even knew what I was missing.

Lorena

It is hard to be a woman up here, yes. It's harder than I could ever begin to tell you, but not for the reasons you are thinking. It was not my body that caused me to suffer when I first came up here. It was not the heavy packs or the cold or the hunger. Physically I have always been strong as a horse, just as you see me now. From the very first day, I took to the mountains like a duck to water. Psychologically, too, I was well-prepared for this life. War did not frighten me, although it saddened me, as it saddens all of us. This was not the problem either. My father had taught me well before he sent me up here. I came prepared, ready for what I would find in this new life. The problems lay in my notions of what a woman should or shouldn't be, should or shouldn't do, should or shouldn't think. These things my culture had taught me, my neighbors, my school mates, the people of my small *ladino* town. These were things that my father, as a man, had not foreseen. He was a good revolutionary and a kind father, but he did not understand about women, and so he could not protect me from the things that lay ahead.

I was seventeen when I arrived up here. In the first months, there was much to learn. Since I was from a town instead of the country, I had to get used to working with a machete, to cut poles for a tent, to build a fire, to differentiate the sounds of the night when I stood post. This kept me much too busy to miss my home very much. And I had always been a very independent person, which had made me my father's favorite child. At first I needed no one. But after a few months, I admit, I began to fall in love with one of the *compañeros*. He was much older than I was, mature, experienced, and very sweet with me always. He had such simple ways, and was not a proud person at all, even though he was the one in the camp who really knew the most. He was able to guide me, and share what he knew with me, without ever making me feel foolish. He helped me to grow up, I realize now, when I remember him. His name was Daniel.

We were quietly sweethearts for many months. Quietly, so as not to make the others feel their own loneliness, and also because I was very afraid of having a true relationship with him. I was such a child still, in that way. I was so afraid of loosing my virginity, terrified, actually. It had nothing to do with Daniel, for I truly loved him. And it had nothing to do with my father either. It had to do with the culture I was raised in. You have no idea how much baggage I came up here with, mentally. In my town, it was a terrible sin to have sex before marriage; only very bad girls would do that. Any man who asked such a thing was certainly not to be trusted. And my girl friends would whisper so many things about the sex not one of us knew about—how badly it would hurt the first time, how much blood there would be. The idea of a woman living as freely as a man never entered our heads. We women have to rid ourselves of so many of the old ideas when we come into the movement. We have to free not only our country, but ourselves as individuals, as well. And this is what I was going through, for many months.

Daniel understood me. He too, after all, had grown up in a city, and had gone through many changes of his own when he first entered the movement. There was a time when he, too, would have considered a woman who had sex before marriage to be undeserving of respect. And because he himself had changed so many of his own views about women, he was able to understand what I was going through, why I was so afraid. He also understood that I was terribly young. And so we talked and talked, and Daniel waited for me, until I was truly ready to be with him, unafraid. And of course that time finally came. I went to his tent one cold night and did not leave. After that I was his *compañera,* and he was my *compañero,* and we were both very happy. We did everything together, from combat to cooking. I was sure we would be together for another fifty years at least, but he never commented on this idea. He had been at war for too long.

Our relationship was very smooth, very happy, for a long time, probably thanks to Daniel's maturity and patience. Really, we almost never quarrelled. But after about six months, I became pregnant. I didn't know what was wrong at first, I just felt tired and nauseous all the time, and thought I must have parasites or anemia. Daniel was really worried about me and finally talked me into going to the platoon physician. That is how we found out that I was pregnant. This, of course, is the one thing that cannot be up here. Sexual relations are allowed, because we are all human beings, and deserve to live as human beings. But we must be very responsible. We cannot trifle with one another or hurt each other. We must have respect for one another. And we women cannot stay in the mountains if we are pregnant. It simply is not safe. The choice of solutions is for the individual to make. She can have an abortion, or she can go down from the mountains to have her child, and she can either stay down, or leave the child with a relative and return to combat. Her *compañero* can accompany her or stay in the mountains, as they choose. The most basic decision though, is the woman's. And that decision is difficult. I know.

Daniel was as dismayed as I was. We had taken the correct precautions, but here I was pregnant anyway. He was completely loyal to me, of course, and tried to work through the possible solutions, step by step. But somehow, I blamed him, even though this was so unfair. He was the one who had talked me into sex, who had made me trust him. Now I was the one with the problem, not him. The fear and pain made me angry, and in my anger I said many things that I know must have hurt Daniel terribly. He never rebuked me, though. He just stayed with me until I decided to go down to the city for an abortion. He held my hand and supported me as much as I would allow him to, but I left, furious and in tears.

The experience of the abortion only made things worse. I was so ashamed, sitting in that small dark waiting room, under false papers declaring me to be a married woman. All the old ideas came back in a rush in that environment, all those old notions of sin and shame and punishment. The room smelled of stale cigarettes, and on the dirty wall was a framed drawing of Jesus, son of the virgin Mary. Can you imagine how I felt there?

I returned to the mountains healthy enough but saddened. It took a long time for my relationship with Daniel to heal. Once again, he waited for me, and tried to ease me through my hard times. But I had a lot of anger towards him, unfair but real. It hurts me, now, to remember, even though I know he understood and forgave it all. Somehow, this only makes it worse.

It was a few months after the abortion that Daniel left with a small unit for a battle with the enemy. It was routine, and I was not frightened when he left. A battle means a good chance of death, always, but somehow we never allow ourselves to believe it can happen. Or we don't allow ourselves to think about it. Otherwise we could never survive up here, emotionally, at least. Daniel and I embraced when he left, and I told him I loved him, and he held me close. Things had been returning to normal, slowly but surely, between us. Then he shouldered his pack and marched off with the others, turning just once to wave and flash me that kindly smile. I remember that it was raining and that I was worried about the hole in his left boot. That was the last time I ever saw him.

I heard later about how he died. The battle itself had gone well enough. They had captured a number of badly needed weapons and had taken no casualties at all. It was after the battle that the trouble began. They were running through a cornfield, back up towards the slopes of our volcano, when the planes and helicopters arrived, dropping bombs and strafing every inch of the field with machine gun fire. Amazingly, everyone survived the first round of explosions and the group had almost made it to the edge of the forest when the second round began. Shrapnel and bullets were everywhere, and the noise was deafening. Several *compañeros* fell, wounded, and a third round began. Daniel was hit, and the others saw him, running towards the *comandante*, trying to make sure that he was safe. Daniel was bleeding terribly, but his worry was for the others. As he ran, another blast of shrapnel struck him, and he fell down, his skull torn open. This was the last round of gunfire. After that, the planes left and the field was silent. The other *compañeros* ran to where Daniel had fallen and found him dying there, quiet but very clear-minded. He refused to let them try and bandage him up, telling them to first go find the others, who had a chance of surviving. Then he gave away the things in his pack, the food, the blanket, his small book. He was writing a note, shaken but determined, when they left him. The note was for me, but I never received it.

When Roberto came to where I was waiting to tell me what happened, my heart stopped for a moment. For a moment I did not know where I was or what day I was living. I was just blank. Then I ran after Roberto, through the trees, down the steep slopes, trying to reach Daniel before he died. I ran so hard I had no wind in my lungs left for crying. We began to pass the other *compañeros*, carrying the wounded on makeshift stretchers. There were some very bad injuries, but I did not stop to help. The others motioned me down towards the cornfield, telling me to hurry. Roberto and I arrived, breathless, at the place where he had left Daniel, but at first we could see nothing. I thought we must have come to the wrong place, and started to move on when Roberto suddenly jerked me up against him, pulling my face into his shoulder. I struggled free, though, and took two more steps forward, to the scene Roberto had tried to spare me. Daniel was not there. His body had vanished, with his pack, his boots, his book, and the note for me. There on the ground lay only his brain, bloody and intact. The soldiers had found Daniel first.

After some moments, I found myself on my knees, on the soft ground, Roberto's arms wrapped tightly around me. He was weeping, but I was too stunned to weep with him. I kept thinking that I should get up, keep moving, go find Daniel, the real Daniel, wherever he was, go tell him goodbye, and I love you just once more before it was too late. But my arms and legs were like stone, and I could go nowhere. Finally though, I knew what I must do. I pulled out my machete and crawled over to where the brain lay. Then I dug a small hole in the ground, and wrapped the brain in my bandanna. I laid it gently in the hole, and covered it up as neatly as I could with the earth and some small stones to keep the animals away. Then I cut two sticks for a little cross to mark the grave. I would not let Roberto help me. These were the last services I would ever be able to give to Daniel.

For a year, I drifted close to madness. During the day the pain would sweep over me, drowning me, robbing me of my appetite, taking away my strength and will. At night, the dreams would come, visions of that terrible cornfield, leaving me weeping and shaken. The other *compañeros* tried to help me, keeping me close to them, urging special food on me, bringing me to sleep in their tents at night.

They never left me alone. And finally, by the end of the year, I found that I had survived. Just as today, talking with you, I find that I have survived up here for nearly ten years.

So you see now, don't you, why I smile when you ask about the problems for women combatants. Are we big enough? Fast enough? Can we carry a one-hundred-pound pack? Will we cause fights among the men? These are questions for children, and there are no children up here. The real question for all of us, men and women alike, is whether or not we have the emotional flexibility and strength to survive the realities of this terrible war.

Sisifu,
the Commando Squirrel

Christ, they told you to ask me about that awful squirrel? I can't believe it, I absolutely can't believe those *compas*. I bet they're laughing themselves sick over there at the campfire right this minute, aren't they? I can practically hear them from here.

Okay, okay, I admit Sisifu was my squirrel, and that he did cause quite a ruckus up here for a while. But it was not all my fault. Hell, aren't they ever going to let me live it down? I guess not, huh? Here, sit down on the edge of my blanket here, and I'll tell you the whole story. Have some of this *atole* with me while we talk, because it's going to take me awhile to explain everything.

I have always liked animals. I grew up with dozens of pets, you see, everything from parrots to turtles to crazy little dogs I would find in the streets and bring home. My mother wasn't always so happy about my menagerie, but my father humored me in all this. He understood that to me animals were just like people, with their own personalities and likes and dislikes. He would laugh sometimes to hear me talking with my pets in such a serious tone of voice. But I was very responsible, and trained them all well, and took good care of them. This he respected. Only once did I come close to loosing my pet privileges, and that was over a one-eyed parrot. I was absolutely crazy about this bird, and would take him out of his cage all the time to smooth his feathers and try and teach him some words. I would also sleep with him. Sometimes I would sleep with my puppy on one side of the bed, and my parrot on the other. I tell you, I never slept better than in those days. But anyway, I woke up one morning to find my parrot dead in my bed. My sister heard me howling, and came running to see what had happened. We were both very young, and she liked all my pets, too, and understood why I was so upset. So to make me feel better, she offered to help embalm my bird, so I could at least keep him in the cage in my room. This I happily agreed to, so we took the bird apart, stuffed him with sawdust and sewed him back up. I guess we didn't do a very good job though, because after a few days all his feathers fell out and he began to stink. You can guess my mother's reaction when she found the bird like this. Not even my father could say much in my defense then.

So anyway, about Sisifu. You see how it is up here. It's easy to get a little lonely at night, especially if you're single. And I had been missing my family, even though I knew they were fine and approved of what I am doing. And so when I found this little baby squirrel on the ground, you can imagine how delighted I was. He was very tiny; his eyes were still closed, and he didn't have a lot of fur. So I just scooped him up in my hands and rushed him back to my tent. For a week or so, I fed him through an eye dropper until he grew stronger. And of course, he slept with me. He was extremely tame right from the start. I named him Sisifu—who knows why? It just seemed like a good name for a baby squirrel. You should have seen all the other *compañeros*. Even though they tease me to death now about

Sisifu, they were all as crazy about him as I was. My tent was absolutely full of *compas* day and night, all wanting to pet the squirrel, or feed him, or play with him. I never had any time to myself at all back then, but this was fine. I was proud of Sisifu and liked for him to be properly appreciated.

The only problem was that Sisifu was so cute and funny as a baby that we all got used to spoiling him rotten. Down in the kitchen area, the *compas* would give him bits of corn and pet him; in the tents he would get crackers; up at the posts, everyone would toss him a bit of the *tamales* they had saved from breakfast. He got used to thinking that all food belonged to him, as a birthright, more or less. After all, that was the way we were treating him. I began to worry and warned the other *compas* that we had to change our ways, reminding them that Sisifu was a squirrel, not a cat or a dog. He couldn't be house-broken or trained later. No one would listen, though. They were all having too much fun playing with our baby squirrel. I knew trouble was coming, but I had no idea how much.

Well, Sisifu grew up into quite a bad teenager. He no longer needed us to feed him, thank you. He was quite able to help himself to any food he wanted. He scavenged the kitchen regularly, gobbling up anything left unprotected, from corn to sugar to wild roots. He wasn't particular. We thought we had resolved the problem by covering everything up, but no, this did not stop Sisifu one bit. I came back from hauling water one day when I was on kitchen duty, only to find him swimming around in our cauldron full of tamales, nibbling and enjoying himself as if he were in a great big bathtub. That really did it as far as I was concerned. I jerked him out of there by the back of the neck and gave him a good spanking. I knew this wouldn't work, but really, what else could I do? I couldn't let him go on thinking that the platoon food all belonged to him. We were willing to share with him, but we had to eat too, after all. Sisifu didn't take kindly to discipline, though. He fled shrieking to the trees and would not come back for hours.

The other *compas* started trying to train him, too, pushing him away from the food, stamping their boots to stop him, or making smacking noises with a rolled up paper. Nothing worked, of course. It was too late. In the end Sisifu just flew into a rage and took to the trees once and for all. He wouldn't come out or make friends again no matter how much we pleaded and coaxed.

The problem was, he wouldn't stay in the trees. He wouldn't come out for us any more, but he sure did come out for food, and with a vengeance. He started making sneak attacks on the *compas'* tents while they were away, making off with their extra rations. Nothing was safe, no matter how careful we were. If you turned your back on your tent for even three minutes, Sisifu would take note and make one of his lightning raids. We couldn't ever catch him, or even see him in action, he was so fast and so shrewd. All we would see were the squirrel prints in the mud and his teeth marks on whatever the food had been wrapped in. You could tell that this squirrel had been raised by subversives—he was sneakier and faster than all the rest of us put together. The *comandante* joked that at least he was a respectful subversive. After all, Sisifu had never violated his tent. I guess Sisifu was listening, though, because that very afternoon, the *comandante's* stash of chocolate disappeared into thin air, with only a crumpled wrapper left on the ground as evidence. Ruefully, we promoted Sisifu to the rank of honorary commando. He deserved it.

Finally that squirrel just went too far. I came home after a long day on the trails to find that he had eaten a big hole through my windbreaker to get at the crackers I had tied inside. What's more, he was sitting just a few feet away, clutching a bit of cracker in his paws and smirking at me. That did it. That absolutely did it. I don't know how I moved so fast, but I managed to grab Sisifu by the neck before he could take to the trees. He must have been weighed down by all the food he'd been stealing. He certainly had been getting fat. I held on for dear life even when he bit me. He was definitely outraged. As I hauled him down to the kitchen he was chattering away in an ear-splitting shriek. No way was I going to let go, though. He had been too bad for words. I called to all the other *compañeros* and they came running, all of them amazed to see that I had actually captured the squirrel. We locked him in a box for a while and tried to decide what on earth to do about him. After all, he had been our pet, and it was our own fault for spoiling him, so killing him was out of the question. We still had a little soft spot for him, in spite of everything.

In the end, we decided to cut his claws short, so he couldn't rip into our supplies so easily. He bit me again while we did this, but I couldn't blame him and didn't hold a grudge. I just wanted him to leave our supplies alone. I even left a little food out for him near my tent, to show him no hard feelings, but for days he wouldn't come near it. He just sat in the trees nearby, shrieking his rage out every time I passed close to him. The absolute end came one day when we were playing soccer in a small clearing. He was sitting high above us, hurling down squirrel insults at us, and we were laughing, half playing with the ball, half watching him. All of a sudden he slipped, and between his big belly and his short claws, he couldn't get a good grip on the branch. After a heroic struggle, he came crashing down among us and sat stunned next to the soccer ball, his eyes red with fury. We couldn't help but laugh at the sight, and he took off wildly into the bushes, as if we had been pulling his tail out. And of course, as soon as his claws grew back, no crumb of food was safe from him. There was nothing for us to do but get used to it. After all, we raised him.

After a while, it was time to move base camps. As we packed up our belongings, I couldn't help but look around for him, hoping for a final goodbye chatter. But he was nowhere in sight. I worried about him. Once we were gone, would he find enough food on his own? I had saved an entire breakfast *tamal* just for him, and I crumpled it up on the ground near where my tent had been. I knew he would come for it later, and hoped it would at least give him a good start in his new life. As we marched off, I felt a little twinge of sadness, because bad as he was, Sisifu had one hell of an interesting personality. I can't help but miss him still, all these years later.

Lucia
and the
Circle of San Pablo

It was such a very terrible dream. I woke up gagging with rage and fright. It was still well before dawn, but I had to sit up to ease the pounding in my head. We had been on a long march for the last few days and had pitched camp quite late the night before, so I was very tired—too tired to get up, yet too upset to go back to sleep. I had dreamed that we were all dying.

For a while I tossed and turned, trying to stay warm under my thin blanket. It was still so cold and dark and silent. The others were deep in an exhausted sleep, so I rolled closer to a nearby *compa* and comforted myself by listening to his even breathing. Later, as it grew lighter, I stumbled up and wandered towards the sentry post, looking for someone to talk to. Our unit had some seventy combatants, and they were all spread out in the small clearing, fully dressed, their boots on their feet, their packs and rifles only inches from their fingertips. In those days, even asleep, you had to be ready to fight for your life. You could never relax, never lower your guard. Otherwise, you wouldn't have a life to fight for.

As I picked my way across the sleeping bodies of my friends, I came upon the *comandante*. He, too, had awakened early and was sitting quietly under a tree, making notations on a scrap of paper. Still uneasy, I stumbled over to his side and began to tell him of my dream, and how it had awakened me from a sound sleep. I told him of the terrible rain of bullets, and how I had seen us all falling, dying. He began to reassure me, patting my arm, explaining that he had just spoken with the sentry and that all was well. Sitting next to him in the brightening light, I began to feel much better. After all, it was only a dream. He had me laughing a few minutes later over some crazy story, and by the time we started talking about my new responsibilities with the unit radio, I had almost forgotten my fears. It was then, while the others were just beginning to stir, that it all began.

There was a hideous burst of fire from nearby automatic weapons, not one but many, from all different sides of our encampment. Bullets were pouring into the clearing, churning up the earth, screaming over our heads. The other *compañeros* had leapt to their feet at the first sound, and for a few moments there was chaos as we took the best cover we could and returned fire. But the explosions and the hail of bullets seemed to be coming from everywhere at once. Within minutes, the two *compañeros* to my left lay dead in the mud, cut down by gunfire coming from behind us. One of the sentries returned in despair. During the night the army had quietly encircled us with three concentric rings of soldiers and a fence of barbed wire. Now they were closing in on us with mortars and machine guns. Against my will, I began to weep as I returned fire and reloaded my rifle. I was weeping for the dead, falling steadily around me, for the other sentry who had not returned, and for what I feared was about to come to all of us. I couldn't think of much else but keeping my head down in the midst of the smoke and hot shards of metal hurtling so close by. But the *comandante* has always been a clear thinker and a very calm man. That is why he is the *comandante*, of course. And it is because of his clear head that any of us lived through that day at all. After a few minutes, he called to all of us that we could not stay together and survive, and that we could not stay where we were. He ordered us to break into many small groups and charge the enemy, past the machine guns and past the barbed wire. We had to attack at many different angles and break the circle at one point, at least, if any of us were to live. Needless to say, we did not like this idea very much at all, but we also knew he was right. So we snatched up our packs from the ground, and bid each other hasty goodbyes as we split into several groups. I waved across the clearing to Miguel, who had been my closest friend, and he smiled back, filling me with courage. Then he lowered his head and ran off into the shadows and the noise. I wondered if I would ever see him again. As it turned out, I never did, for he died that afternoon.

I ended up in a group of five other *compañeros*. The *comandante* was with us, and Chejo, our doctor, and Julia and Martin, a young couple who had come to the mountains together, and Beto, an old friend. We would have hesitated, I suppose, before plunging forward into that wall of gunfire, but we knew that to stay where we were meant death, or worse yet, capture and torture. So we lowered our heads and ran, trying to dodge from rock to tree to hillock, anything that could give us a shred of cover.

I don't remember much about those first few minutes. I could barely see; I was terrified, running and ducking—the noise was deafening. There was smoke everywhere, with such an acrid, burning stench. Then suddenly in front of me was a barbed wire fence. I saw the *comandante* throw himself over it and crawl rapidly across the mud on the other side. As I came closer, I brought my feet together and gave a tremendous leap—a leap for my life—and flew over the fence as if I had turned into a dove and sprouted wings. I had the entire radio set up in my pack, and it was incredibly heavy. There had been no time to take it out, and I had dimly thought that we should try to save it. I don't know how I got over that fence with it, but I did. To tell the truth, I didn't even notice the damned radio was there at all.

As I jumped, I shredded my shirt and cut my arm on the barbs, but felt no pain. I just kept running, charging through the smoke and the circles of the soldiers. When at last I broke free, I was not even frightened any more, just filled with a wild joy that I was still alive and out of the circle. I was determined to survive. So I threw myself on the ground, and crawled wildly through the roots and vines and mud until I almost crashed into the *comandante*. He and Chejo were both there, catching their breath and looking at a small river in front of us. They grabbed me and we embraced emotionally. For all I knew, they were the only other *compañeros* left alive. They had seen Beto fall. None of us had seen Julia or Martin, not even at the fence. We could only hope that they were safe somewhere.

We decided that our best chance lay in swimming the river in front of us and running into the

cornfield on the other side, where it would be difficult to see us. As we spoke, a group of soldiers bore
down upon us, shrieking insults and opening fire.
There was no more time to talk, so we threw ourselves down the slippery mud banks and into the
foaming river. As the water closed over my head, I
realized how much colder and deeper it was than I
had expected, with a strong and swift current. I like
to swim, but I was being dragged under with my
heavy pack and battered against the rocks. Bullets
still whined past my head, but the water was slowing down the soldiers as well. I struggled for a while,
trying to drag myself to the other bank, tiring. As I
was thrown against a log I wrapped my arms
around it, gasping for air. On the other side, all I
could see were the *comandante's* hands, the rest of
him was submerged. For a moment, I thought he
had drowned. As I shouted out his name, though,
he came up for air. He had ducked under to escape
a spray of bullets. Together, we made it to the other
side, dragging each other, hanging on to one another as if we were life rafts. It took a very long time,
but finally we were lying, exhausted, on the muddy
banks. We would have lain there for a while, I suppose, but the soldiers had heard me when I called
out the *comandante's* name, and there was no one
in all of Guatemala they would have liked more to
capture. The few who had run after us had called
for reinforcements, and now there were half a dozen
thrashing their way across the river, and many
more on the other bank, shooting at us. They were
shouting at each other not to let the *comandante*
escape, to go after him no matter what and not to
loose him. So we staggered to our feet and ran on.

Life in the Revolution

Not far into the cornfield we found Chejo, on his knees and covered with blood. He was waiting for us, and from his face we all knew that he was dying. He had taken a very bad wound to the abdomen. We grabbed him under the arms and dragged him further and further into the cornfield, begging him to hang on until we could reach a safe place to bandage him up. The *comandante* is a physician himself, and Chejo had been one of his students at the university. As we dragged him, stumbling, I could not stop my tears, for Chejo was a very special *compañero* for all of us. He was everyone's favorite brother, always gentle, always taking care of us, always comforting. He had helped me through so many difficult times, the thought of losing him filled me with despair. As soon as we found a sheltered bit of level ground, we lay him down and tore open his bloody clothes. As the *comandante* worked on him, the soldiers grew closer, and bullets began to strike the ground around us once again.

Chejo was pleading with us to shoot him and run, to save ourselves. He knew he could not survive, but he did not want to be left to the soldiers. He also did not want us to die because of him. So he reached out for his rifle and thrust it at us, begging us to shoot. I couldn't do it, though; I just couldn't. The bullets drove me down into the mud for a moment, and when I looked up, the *comandante* was still working desperately. Then a bullet hit his backpack. He leaped a bit further into the rows of corn, then reached out to drag Chejo with him, motioning for me to help. I knew there was no hope. Chejo was pleading for death. As I crawled towards him, I knew I should shoot him, just as I would want for someone to shoot me, under those circumstances. I looked into his kindly face, into his eyes, my own eyes blinded with tears. Then I reached for his rifle. He didn't give it to me, though. Instead, he smiled weakly at me, turned it around and placed the barrel in his own mouth. Then somehow he managed to halfway sit up, despite his wound, and pull the trigger himself. As always, he had sheltered me. I'm sorry, but remembering this always chokes me up, even though it happened many years ago. Ah, *compañero* Chejo, I will never forget you.

After that, I ran on blindly with the *comandante*. We were both silent, but for our muffled weeping. I was covered with Chejo's blood and brains. We ran on and on, for hours, numb with exhaustion and distress, until, finally, it was nightfall, and we had left the soldiers far behind us. We threw ourselves down in a thicket of vines and leaves, somewhere deep in a forest, and collapsed. I fell asleep with my arms still hanging limply through the loops of my backpack. It was not until the next day that I even noticed the radio equipment, wet but miraculously still functional, that I had carried all the way from that terrible circle.

The *comandante* woke me up early, shaking my arm and asking me how I had slept. Wryly, he told me that if I ever had any dreams again, he wanted to hear about them right away. It was the first time I had laughed since we had joked together under the tree the day before. We stood up slowly, taking stock of our situation, dusting ourselves off. Every bone, every muscle in my body hurt. We drank a little water from a canteen and ate some crackers that he fished out from the bottom of his pack. We were suddenly ravenously hungry, but there was no more food, so we drifted back towards the cornfield, hoping to find some of the other *compañeros* alive. We walked and walked, past the corn plants, over a small group of stones that crossed the now silent river, but we found no one. I was becoming a little nervous, as we came closer and closer to the scene of the battle the day before, but there was no sign of the enemy. Evidently content with the slaughter, they had left the area and moved on. Still, we walked on the balls of our feet, guns at the ready.

Finally, we came across Alfredo. He had been shot through both legs, and had been hidden by a group of villagers in the safety of a small thicket. You can imagine how glad we were to find him alive. We held each other for a long time, crying out each other's names. While the *comandante* checked his wounds, Alfredo told us his story. He had been shot through the knee as he climbed over the fence, then through the thigh as he fell to the ground. Prepared for death, he was surprised when the soldiers ran right over him, chasing after the surviving *compañeros*, and leaving him for dead on the ground. He had lain still for hours, listening to the terrible gunfire and the screams of the wounded, until finally all was quiet. Then he had dared to sit up and bandage his legs as best he could. He had dragged himself from corpse to corpse on the ground, gathering food and medical supplies from the backpacks. He knew, he explained, that someone else would survive and get back to him and that we would all need food. And with that he reached into his pack and brought out some cold tortillas and dried fruit that we all devoured greedily.

173

We hauled Alfredo up and half carried him. He wrapped one arm around each of our necks, and together we staggered forward, with him giving directions about where he had last seen or heard any of the others. We found two more people, wounded but alive, hidden in the trees and then another couple on a ridge above the river. And so the day wore on, small groups of us finding other small groups, and embracing, exclaiming. There were five more down near the river, another three hidden in a nearby village. Our numbers grew and grew, as did our spirits. There were many wounded but alive, and we moved on to a safer place to pitch a camp and rest. As the days passed, we regained more and more surviving *compañeros*. Each one we welcomed with joy and fierce embraces. By the end of the week, we were nearly fifty in number again. More than twenty had died, a number that we were to grieve for a very long time. Many more were badly hurt. But fifty of us were miraculously alive. To this day, I don't know how so many of us were able to escape with our lives. It still seems impossible. So much of this whole war has seemed impossible at times, yet here we are, many years later, stronger than ever. Here I am, telling you this crazy story.

We were glad to be alive, but still, we were badly shaken, and badly depressed over the loss of our friends. Even those of us who were not wounded wandered about looking pale and lost. This was natural enough, but it was not good. Finally, after enough time had gone by for a good rest, the *comandante* gathered us all together. He told us we were all pale and dispirited and moping around like a bunch of limp newborns, and that the time had come for us to get our spirit back. There was word that the enemy was going to be passing through a nearby area, where it would be easy to ambush them. It was time to regain our courage, time to get our packs on and move. And so we did. We went down to the where the army was headed and set up an ambush for them and fought a pitched battle that lasted for days. Needless to say, we won hands down. At first I was skittish, frightened, but as I fought, all my strength came back to me in a flood, and I fought with a wild inspiration. All of us felt that way, I think, even the wounded who could only stay at the camp and wait for us to return, this time with good news. It was the only way for us to heal ourselves and go on.

And we have gone on, as you can see. Ever since that day I have been in charge of the radio communications for our unit. When the rest of the *compañeros* found out that I had leaped over that fence and ran and swam with all that radio gear in my pack, and hadn't even noticed the extra weight, they laughed for days. And when they stopped laughing, it was unanimously decided that I deserved my new position. And so here you have found me, at my switchboard all these years later.

Nicolas,
as Remembered
by Jennifer

When I first met Nicolas he had a plastic bag over his head, with tiny holes cut out for his eyes, nose, and mouth. He was standing on a rough street barricade thrown up in haste in front of the university, speaking out against the repression even as the tanks rolled down the streets towards us. Not surprisingly, I did not recognize him when he stopped me near my hotel, winking, a few days later. In return for his kindly smile, I sent him a rude frown, and it was only after he chased me for several blocks, trying discreetly to remind me of where we had met, that I realized who he was. Later, long after we had become inseparable, he would tell this story to our friends and laugh, shaking his finger at me in mock displeasure.

Nicolas had a baby from a previous marriage, a small son of about two, with the same large brown eyes and delicate hands as his father's. In a rash and youthful moment, he had been named after a famous revolutionary, but now, given the realities in the city, his family had taken to calling him Angel. He was the apple of Nicolas' eye. Round and solemn, he would appear every Saturday at my door, hand in hand with his father, and together we would walk to the small mercado to find him a new wind-up toy. They were cheap and fragile, not made to survive a two-year-old's hands, but I remember that they were very ingenious. There was a monkey that clanged a very loud little bell, and, perhaps the favorite, a rolling hamburger that stuck out a bright red tongue with a pasted-on slice of tomato.

Nicolas knew of every new word, every bump and scrape, every new tooth that Angel could produce. His friends laughed and accused him of being an addled parent. I never laughed, though, because I knew the whole story of Nicolas and Angel. How not long ago, Nicolas had gone to political meetings with a couple named Rosario and Carlos. Angel had gone, too, to play with their little son Augustin. Rosario and Carlos are now long dead. Carlos' body was never found; Augustin was buried next to his mother, with his broken neck and missing fingernails. I knew that our time was too brief for teasing and for questions. So I searched for ever better wind-up toys, and gave Nicolas the key to my room whenever I left town. I knew, without asking, that he needed a safe place for times of trouble. And I helped as best I could with other small things: keeping unmarked packages, standing at certain corners at certain times of day, taking telephone messages, word for word, that I could not understand. This, and my love for them both, was all I had to offer.

Nearly a year passed in this way, quietly but with much unspoken fear. Nicolas would be a day late, and I would sob, wondering if he was dead, captured at last, knowing there was no one to call. I could only wait for the newspapers, or a mysterious voice on the phone, sorrowful but brief, then the click of disconnection. It was on one night like this, as I tried to distract myself with a cheap Mexican soap opera, that I heard his light steps, not walking, but running up the back stairwell, and another, heavier step not far behind him. I threw open the door, thinking he was being pursued, and he bounded in, together with a very young and worried-looking friend. Nicolas introduced the friend as Pancho, a sure sign I should ask no questions. I bolted the door carefully and checked the streets below my window.

Pancho was tearing off his shirt and rifling through my closet, tossing out my unisex clothing to Nicolas. They smiled at each other, and thanked God aloud for *gringo* clothing styles. I produced scissors and a small shaver, and they quickly cut their hair and removed their beards and mustaches, jostling elbows in front of my small mirror. I asked if everything was alright, and Nicolas turned, lather-faced and rather sheepish, wondering aloud why I would have such thoughts.

It was at that moment that the first knock sounded, harsh and jarring, on my flimsy door. We stopped laughing, and Nicolas, pale, signaled for Pancho to be silent. A little too loudly, I asked who was there, and an angry, masculine voice answered curtly that I should open the door, that I would not be hurt. It was a voice that made my mouth go dry, a voice that all along, I had been waiting for and dreading. Pancho and Nicolas looked quietly at one another, and embraced. "It's our turn," Nicolas said, and the two shook their heads sadly towards me. Then they opened my small window and crowded together atop the ledge. They did not even glance down to the plate glass sun roof of the coffee shop four floors below. There was no need for them to look—they knew what lay below, and chose it.

Nicolas took Pancho's hands, and they sat, waiting.

"Who's there!" I yelled through the door, wanting to break it down, to flatten out the person on the other side. I could feel only rage that some mad stranger could stalk these two young people to my room, and drag them away to secret, horrible deaths, as though they had never existed. Rage that there was no way to stop him, or even to bring him to justice; rage at my own helplessness. Why had I never brought Nicolas the gun he had asked me for?

On the other side of the door, the deep voice repeated that I should open up, that I would not be hurt. Nicolas, expecting bullets, gestured me away from the door, leaving me filled with despair. "Who's there?" I screamed again. "Answer me now! I'm all by myself here, and if you don't go away I am going to call the police!"

From the ledge, Nicolas rolled his eyes. "Foolish one!" he hissed at me, "That is the police!". He could not stop me, though. I tried one last time, my voice breaking. "Who's there, who are you, why are you bothering me?" And finally the deep-voiced man answered again, this time in a noticeably drunken tone, that he was staying in a room down the hall, that someone kept banging on his wall, was it me who was doing this? He was trying to sleep. He was very angry, but not anywhere near as angry as I was. I shouted for him to leave me alone, and he finally shuffled away, telling me not to be so touchy.

Once we were sure that he was gone, I sank down on the bed, crying. Nicolas and Pancho climbed out of the window, shaking their heads ruefully and stretching their cramped legs. They looked at each other, then finally burst out laughing.

Nicolas was the first to speak. "Let's shoot him," he suggested, making me laugh with him. We joked, for awhile then, trying to calm our frayed nerves. I sneaked down to the cafe to bring back three small bottles of beer which Nicolas normally would not drink. We toasted another day and spent the night talking and telling funny stories together, huddled on the floor under my thin, spare blankets.

And so the two of them survived a little longer in the ever tightening sweep of the city. But not very much longer. Nicolas had to leave for the mountains, his heart breaking to leave his small son. I don't know where he is today, or if he is still alive. Pancho survived only ten more days. Determined that the death squads should never take him alive, he took to riding a motorcycle through the crowded city streets. When the black-windowed cars came after him, he led them on a mad but hopeless chase, then drove, without a moment's hesitation, under the wheels of an enormous truck, crushing his body but escaping, once and for all, the fate his enemies had prepared for him.

Everardo

Women have been up here in the mountains, in combat, since the very beginning. They fight bravely, they work hard, and they contribute good ideas. It is right that they are here. They are half of our country and half of our revolution. Sometimes there are complications, but these arise from love and from our difficult reality. I am not talking about small quarrels and petty jealousies. I am talking about pain. For a man to lose his *compañera* is a terrible wound, but it is also terrible to lose a brother. The relations are different but the pain and the sadness are the same. I know, because I have been here for more than fifteen years, and I have grieved for both.

Like many of the *compañeros*, I grew up on a plantation. My family is Mayan, so, of course, we were not the owners, only the serfs. My father labored long, hard hours in the fields just to keep us alive. My mother died of illness when I was very young; we had no money for doctors and medicines. I don't have many memories of my mother, but I remember that in the years after her death, there was no one in the house to feed us while my father was away, and that my sisters and I suffered hunger. My father did the best he could and moved us into an aunt's house, hoping that she would care for us while he labored, but she was not happy to have more mouths to feed. If we gathered firewood and did other chores, she would give us food, but always with a slap and a shout, or a cuff to the ears. After a while, I stopped going to her for food. I pre-

181

ferred hunger to her unfairness and would wait outside all day until my father returned from the fields. He watched me growing thinner and thinner, and knew the reason without questioning me. So every night he would ask if I had eaten yet, and would take me with him to the table to eat in peace. More than this, he could not do for me.

As I grew older, I wanted to go to school. I like to learn things, to know things, and I wanted badly to go, to learn to read and write. My young cousin went to a nearby schoolhouse for a few years, but I could not go with her. My father taught me the two letters he knew himself, but this was my only education. I had to go to the fields instead—fields that were not even ours—and labor like a mule for pittance wages. This was harder for me than the hunger, not being able to go to school, not being able to learn. And so I grew up restless, angry, and very strong.

By the time I was sixteen or so, I began to run away to the mountains instead of going to the fields. I just wanted time to think, time to be a person instead of a donkey. Sometimes my friends would go with me, to explore a little, and to talk. It was on one of these days that we met Gaspar Ilom and his small group of *compañeros*. This was long before ORPA existed openly. These were the formative years, the years that they were organizing clandestinely, the years that they were building their political base with the people. We had heard of them, of course, as had many other villagers. Their existence was one of the many secrets our people kept from the authorities.

I remember that first day well. Gaspar Ilom was

impressive. Even so very long ago, you could see what kind of a man he was. I liked the others, too. They spoke with us as though we were intelligent people, sharing their ideas, asking for ours. They understood so well the reality that the rest of us were living. I especially liked a *compañero* named Luis Ixmata. We talked all afternoon, and a few days later, I found myself wandering back up the trails, looking for them, wanting to talk more. I went back and back again, thinking about new ideas, things I wanted to tell them about. These were the people who taught me to read and write, who taught me history, and who gave me books. You can imagine what they meant to me, and how I loved them. And so it was that before dawn on my eighteenth birthday, I ran away from home once and for all, up the dark trails, to join Gaspar Ilom's fledgling organization. That was more than fifteen years ago. I never saw my family again, although often I have thought of them. My father was a good and decent man, truly. But I have never regretted my decision. Pain, yes, I have suffered, but doubts, never.

In the early years, I fought in Luis Ixmata's front. We were badly armed, with never enough bullets and rifles that either didn't shoot at all or shot crooked. We were cold and hungry most of the time, and the army was always after us, hunting us. We lost many people, many good people. And yet in other ways, I was very happy. I was learning so much and so quickly, and finally there was a way for me to change a reality I had always detested— the exploitative, unjust reality that our people have faced for the last five hundred years. I talked all the time with Luis Ixmata and grew very close to him. It was during those hard times that he showed himself to be a truly exceptional human being. He was a *ladino*, yet his manners were very simple and sincere. He never put himself above us or gave himself airs, so it was an easy thing for all of us to trust and love him, as we knew he loved and trusted us. The man never tired or grew discouraged, no matter how difficult our situation. For me, he became a second father, a man who would help me with my studies, talk to me about my innermost thoughts and questions. It was with Luis's encouragement that I began to write poetry.

Luis Ixmata, of course, is long dead. They killed him there in the capital more than ten years back, but even now I can see his face so clearly, hear his voice. How pleased he would be to see all the changes, how far down the road towards freedom we have come. What a warm hug he would have for us all. And yet I know what he would say, how he would lecture us about how much more lay ahead, how much more we had to give to our people. If he were here, that's what he would be thinking about, how to give more.

The night I learned Luis was dead, I had to sit down and weep. Him, I had truly loved. There had been so many deaths by then, and they all hurt me, but somehow I had learned to accept what could not be changed. But Luis Ixmata was different, and his death hurt me to the core as it hurts me still. I wept late into the night, for the father, friend and teacher he had been for me. Then I wrote a poem, just for him. I carry it with me to this day, but rarely show it to anyone else. That poem is between me and Luis.

Life in the Revolution

With time, up here, you become very strong because you must. You cannot let a death destroy you because death is so close to each and every one of us. When a *compañero* fell, I learned to understand, to accept the sacrifice willingly given. I learned to have perspective and resilience. I could love, but without any hopes of permanence or possession. I began to take strength from the deaths instead of pain. To remember what had been given by the others helped me to carry on. I learned.

With Gabriela, though, it was very difficult to keep this perspective. She was my first love, and I gave her my heart completely, just as she gave hers to me. I first noticed her at one of our discussion sessions, when she spoke up so very simply, yet with so much intelligence. She had been studying law, down in the city, when she had entered our organization, and it had not taken her long to decide to come up to the mountains to fight. She was very clear minded and mature, and very hard working. I liked her face immediately, open and sweet, with dark steady eyes and curly light hair. Back then it was prohibited to have relations with the *compañeras*. We were afraid that this would lead to complications and fights. It was only later that we learned that relations, in the end, strengthened us instead of weakening us. And so for a long time, Gabriela and I were steadfast friends and *compañeros*, but nothing more, even though we were very much in love. With time, though, our humanity overcame our discipline, and like the other furtive couples, we began to watch for quiet moments to steal away to some private place. And so we became lovers.

We were together for only six months, but these were very intense months indeed. We lived through so many new and different things together: the growth of our unit, our expansion into new and larger areas. Things were changing fast, and we were changing together. It was difficult and yet so exhilarating. We went through villages together, talking to the people, we fought side by side, we whispered late into the night about all of our thoughts and ideas and observations. She gave me so much strength, Gabriela. With her I was strong and complete no matter what happened to us.

It was in a small village that I lost her. We had gone to speak to the people, tell them who we were and why we were fighting, to share our ideas with them, to answer any questions. The people had received us well and were speaking freely with us when the army arrived. I don't know how they knew of our presence, but they arrived suddenly, and with great force. The air was filled abruptly with smoke and the sound of screams and explosions. Machine gun fire was everywhere. Our small group scattered, running through the narrow village streets, and of course, Gabriela and I ran together. At first, though startled, I was confident that we would escape, but after only a few moments, I realized that we were in very serious trouble. The soldiers were much too close and no matter how desperately we ran, the smoke and the shrapnel and bullets were getting closer and closer.

A piece of metal tore into my chest, slowing me down, and I realized that our turn had come to die. I was not so unwilling, but Gabriela would not let me give up. She seized my arm and was running with me, dodging around the twisting streets, urging me onwards. She gave me her strength. We were nearly to the edge of the village when a bullet pierced her leg. She was badly hurt but still, she ran with me, refusing to give up. She was just behind me, and I reached out for her hand.

She was smiling her encouragement to me. And then another bullet struck her, through the heart, stopping her forever. Amid the dust and the smoke and the roar and whine of the explosions, she lay dead in the street, beyond my reach, beyond my rescue.

As you see, I survived. I got out of that village and recovered from my physical wounds. But it was a very long time before I recovered from the death of Gabriela. For more than year, I thought my depression would crush me as hunger and bullets had never been able to. And yet I knew that this she would never have accepted. She would have wanted me to keep going, to keep fighting, to keep pushing onwards until the final triumph for our people. She would have wanted me to be strong, even happy, without her, not suffering as I was. I would have wanted the same for her. All this I understood, and with time, I was able to change my agony to strength and resolve. Even so, the scar left by her death runs very deep. All these years later, it still hurts me to speak of Gabriela.

If Luis and Gabriela were here, they would be the first to protest that their deaths were the same as all the others, that their sacrifices were the same as those of all the other *compañeros* who have given their lives. And this, of course, is true. All those who have fallen are remembered, and are with us still in our hearts, as we draw closer to the end of this long, long war. There are so many others I could tell you of, but there is not enough time. I only speak now of Gabriela and Luis so as to answer your question about women in combat. Of course the death of a woman strikes us very hard. But so does the death of a *compañero*. The bonds forged among us up here are very strong, as is the love we share for one another. Every loss is a very bad loss, be it a man or a woman. The pain, the wound, comes not from the gender, but from love itself. Have I answered your question?

The Model Villages, as Remembered by Jennifer

It was not a happy village. Located in the middle of a malarial swamp, it was ringed with barbed wire and occupied by the army. To a foreigner lucky enough to gain permission for a visit, first from the central military base, then from the soldiers at the end of the dirt road, welcome signs consisted of the charred remains of homes and meeting halls burned long ago. From those former years no villagers remained. Only one lone building, perched on the hilltop, had survived this period. Once the church, it now housed army officers. Stripped of its cross, it served well as a lookout post, not against invading guerrilla forces, but against the villagers themselves.

I had been to this place before and knew some of its history. The soldiers had given me their official story, and the inhabitants, whispering late at night through the window of my hut, had told me theirs. Not surprisingly, the two versions collided. The handsome young officer who escorted me through the village and offered me a lemonade made from bottled water, gave me a well-organized briefing. The original village had been burned by the guerrillas, he explained, and the inhabitants had run off to some other place. The army, seeking to reconstruct this ruined area, had rebuilt the village out of humanitarian concern for the poor locals. A new

189

group of settlers had arrived and begun to clear the abandoned land. Once every two weeks, each man did three hours of volunteer guard duty in the civil patrol, to be sure that the guerrillas could not come back and hurt anybody again. The soldiers, the brothers of the people, were here to give protection and aid.

The villagers told a different story, although always out of the earshot of the soldiers. This was easier said than done since I was followed everywhere by armed and uniformed men. The women would have to take me bathing at the river, where we could not be accompanied, or the men would have to creep past my window at four a.m., as if on their way to the latrine. There was no chance for a long or comfortable conversation, but only bits and snips of information, to be confirmed by others, and then pieced together into a coherent account.

The villagers, it seemed, were the third generation of settlers here. The first generation had come nearly twenty years earlier, led by a priest, in search of land and survival. Here they found acreage that no one else could use or wanted, and they had worked hard to clear the thickets and build a community. With time, and the help of the good priest, they had flourished, building a school and a clinic and forming a cooperative to purchase agricultural equipment and medical supplies. With their new equipment, they were able to process their own crops and sell at far higher prices to the big companies, which were not at all pleased with this new independence. In the end, the army came, and the priest was murdered. The co-op was accused of communist tendencies, and the leaders disappeared. The village was burned to the ground, and the surviving settlers fled their hard-won home, escaping either to Mexico as refugees, or hiding deep within the jungle.

The army, seeking control of the region, then brought in a new group of settlers, many of them from the same highland region as the first. The land plots of the earlier villagers were declared abandoned and resold to the newcomers, as part of a land reform effort that would keep the wealthy landowners safe from harm. This second generation, however, found the combination of a ruthless mother nature and a ruthless army too much to bear, and by the end of the year, nearly two-thirds of the families had fled, either returning to their original homes or drifting into nearby Mexico. Once again, the lands were declared abandoned and resold to yet a third generation, many of whom were related to the first wave of settlers and who remembered the priest and the cooperative. In desperate need of land, any land, and remembering the promise this place had once held, the people were coexisting, uneasily, with the army.

But coexistence was no simple matter. Anyone caught taking extra clothes to their land plots, in case of rain, could be accused of aiding the guerrillas and shot. Anyone taking an extra ration of food to their land plots could be accused of aiding the guerrillas and shot. Anyone who was not at the flagpole at sundown every night, for roll call and a military lecture on the evils of communism, could be shot. Anyone with a cache of extra medical supplies was in serious trouble with the base and could be shot. Anyone who did not report any suspicious activities by a neighbor, such as a lengthy conversation with myself, would be in serious trouble and could be shot or thrown off their lands. Anyone who did not give twenty-four hours a week free guard duty to the civil patrols, as proof of his patriotic fervor, could be called to the military base for questioning. The standard punishment was twenty-four hours of immersion in a pit filled with cold water. Twenty-four hours a week of free civic duty was also expected and usually came in the form of making food for the soldiers, gathering firewood for the base, or clearing land around the trails to ensure safe passage for the military. No one could leave the village without two permits—one from the base, and one from the civil patrol leader. After sundown, no one could leave the village at all. This last I learned the hard way.

Listening to this story unfold, I felt more and more outraged, for the army was claiming these villages as examples of good humanitarian projects, seeking financial support abroad. Some funding, of course, did arrive, but the people never saw any benefit from it. Thin and sallow, they toiled endlessly and without support. I knew there was a malaria project in existence, but no monies or medicines ever arrived, and the small hut reserved for the health workers remained vacant. The hospital back near the main military base, some four hours walk away, remained filled with patients and doctors, but almost no supplies. During one visit, a physician confided that he was using dental floss in emergency surgeries for lack of any better material. The army had seized it all. The social worker also voiced frustration. Despite recognition for the need of a new cooperative in the village, military permission for him to enter the town was almost impossible to obtain.

And so the days of my visit passed. I listened and waited, played checkers with the soldiers, and bathed with the women. At night I slept in the empty school hut and waited for a low whisper to begin outside the window. I dared take no notes or tapes, for I knew I would be searched when I left. I could only listen intently, then repeat the stories to myself until they were ingrained firmly in my memory. Unfortunately, most of the stories were not easy to forget.

It was on my last day in the village that a small boy came to my hut and asked if I had any aspirin. He explained that his aunt's baby was very ill, and that she had asked for aspirin to bring the fever down. I picked up my first aid kit and struggled up a muddy hill, the boy leading the way, to a small thatched structure. There was a crowd of anxious-looking women outside the low door, and even from a distance, I could hear the rhythmic screams of a baby's voice. I hesitated before entering, looking at the grim faces of the other women, knowing that the situation must be serious. Inside, it took my eyes a moment to adjust to the darkness. But then I saw: on a small table built from poles was a thick woven cloth, and on the woven cloth was a small baby, perhaps four months old. He must have been a pretty child once, for his eyes were large and dark, and thickly fringed with long lashes. But now the eyes were blank, and his small arms and legs looked already lifeless. His belly was hugely swollen, red, and hot to the touch. His skin seemed to be sagging, and I looked at the top of his head, my heart sinking. Under the soft black hair, the head showed a concave spot in the center. I felt one of the little hands and found it ice cold. Nevertheless the tiny fingers closed tightly over mine, pleading. He screamed on every exhale.

I turned to the mother, who was standing next to me, weeping. With a start, I recognized her. She and her husband had come here a year earlier with their children. The eldest had died immediately of fever, the second, a few months later of untreated malaria. This was their only surviving child. The father sat in the hammock, his head in his hands, tears beading the long lashes that so resembled his son's. The mother put a trembling hand on my arm then, asking in a whisper for the aspirin. I relinquished the whole medical kit to her, and then began talking with the other villagers who were crowding around us. All agreed that the baby was dying, but their faces showed only the hopelessness born of hard experience. I suggested that we take the baby to the hospital, back at the base, but they reminded me that it was a four hour walk to the road, and that the merchant's vehicles passed by only in the mornings. Then I thought of the military helicopter. It made the rounds of the villages every day, dropping supplies and picking up soldiers. Surely it could make a stop here, on its way back to the base. The others only stared at me, speechless. But as the baby's pitiful screams continued, the mother silently wrapped him into a blanket and thrust him into my arms.

And so I found myself running down the slope with the baby, towards the old church where the soldiers now lived. As I ran, I called out for the handsome young officer. As it happened, he was playing soccer on the nearby field, and called the game to a halt for a moment as I came stumbling towards him. At first he seemed friendly enough, smiling his welcome, but his expression changed as I held out the child for him to see. By now the baby was convulsing, but the officer seemed unmoved. He pointed out that the child was dying and that I should take him back to his home. I begged for the helicopter. He refused the request with anger. I demanded medicine, and he became angrier. We quarreled then, on the field, me reminding him that he was a brother of the people and here to serve, he warning me that there was a war going on. The baby screamed pleas for help. Abruptly, the soldier turned on his heel and stormed back to his game. He and the others continued playing, surrounded by the villagers assigned to guard them as they played. The soldiers' weapons lay in an evil-looking pile near the goal posts.

A crowd had gathered by the side of the field, surrounding me and the weeping mother. The other women, maddened by the child's shrieks, were weeping also, the men shrugging their shoulders in despair. We talked of saddling a horse, but it would soon be nightfall, and no one was allowed to leave the village at night. We talked of my riding out with the child and the problem of not knowing the password, of being shot in the darkness by an uneasy patrol.

As we spoke I held the child tightly in my arms. He had moved his cold little arms slightly, trying to reach towards me, and his fingers had become entangled in my hair. He was still screaming, although his voice was becoming hoarse and weak. I don't believe he could see any longer through those dark, dimming eyes. They were focused on some spot far away. Yet his fingers managed to tug weakly at my hair, and this I could hardly bear. He was so clearly pleading for help, for one of us to save his life. The soldiers were still playing soccer on the field when he died, strangling and spitting blood. His mother took him from me, then, cuddling him close and smoothing shut his dark and pleading eyes.

The evening passed grimly. We returned to the hut to wash the tiny body and lay it, decked with flowers, in a small wooden box. The soldiers came, wreathed in weapons, to rebuke the parents for not asking them for help sooner. If they had come sooner, they explained, watching my face, perhaps the child could have been saved. The parents bowed their heads in submission and nodded. A prayer service was held, the house overflowing with the other villagers, the sound of hymns filling the evening air until very late into the night. The next day was the burial, the little body placed in a shallow grave on a hillside outside of the village. The only marker was a small wooden cross hammered in place with a stone.

I stayed up on the hill for a while, thinking. It was a quiet day, village life going on about me as if nothing had happened, as if yesterday had been normal. Perhaps, for them, the events had, in fact, been quite normal. I closed my eyes for a moment, trying to forget the child's face. When I opened them I saw the mother, standing just above me on a slope not far away. Across her shoulders she carried a sling for two large jars of water from the river. She was not moving, though. Instead, she was staring fixedly towards the old church, now home to the army. Gone was the bland and submissive expression from the day before. Now, in her secret moment, her features were a study of rage and hate. Looking past her into the jungle, I could only wonder about the rebel forces so close by, as the day of reckoning moved inexorably closer. Looking back at the mother, it was so easy to imagine her picking up a gun.

Tomás

We did not lose all of the battles, not even way back then, when we had nothing. It is true that for a long time we had no guns, no bullets, no food, no medicine. It was not like it is now, as you are seeing us, with our good equipment and supplies. The early days were hard, and we survived because of the brains and the courage of all of the *compañeros*. We lost many people, many good people, but we also had victories, even then, under the worst conditions. This helped us to keep our faith. It helps me still, today, to remember what our people were able to achieve. I will tell you about one of those victories, and you can tell me what you think about it.

In Guatemala, there are many ruins left behind by our ancestors. They were built long before the conquistadors ever arrived here on our lands, and they exist still. Some are known to everyone, like the ruins of Tikal, up in the jungles of the Peten. But there are many others that only our people know about that we have never shared with the city people or the foreigners. The secrets of their location and history have been passed down to us from generation to generation, for the last five hundred years. One of these places is an old Mayan fortress where our ancestors fought against the invading Spaniards because they did not wish to be taken into slavery. They lost, for they had no guns or cannon or armor, but they did not ever forget the idea of freedom. This they passed down to us, together with the legend of the fort. To outsiders, it is just an old pile of boulders, but for us it was much more, for we knew the secrets and strategies of its use.

It was during a particularly difficult period that one of our younger *compañeros* remembered this old fortress, and we climbed deep into the mountains to find it. It was not hard to locate—it was just as the boy's grandfather had described it. It was, though, quite hard to reach, for it was located on a very steep cliff with only two narrow footpaths for entries on either side of the site. The footpaths wound around the face of the cliff, straight down on one side and straight up on the other, and they were only wide enough to permit a single file line of people to walk them. Even then, one had to walk very slowly and carefully to avoid going over the edge.

We arrived just as the sun was going down and sat among the ancient boulders for a while, thinking about those who had been there before us. Like all of the old places, there was something special there, something that moved us and gave us strength. We waited until it grew dark, enjoying the few moments of rest and the view down the sharp, green cliffside. Then we got to work.

That night we did many things that as guerrillas we were never able to do. First, we built a big, bright fire and cooked up a good dinner, never minding the visibility of the flame and smoke. We ate well, then turned up our favorite music station on the radio as loud as we wanted. We made a great deal of noise, making no effort at all to hide it. While the music played, we dug deep trenches under some of the biggest boulders, deep enough for several people to fit in. These we reinforced to make strong. It was a big job and took many hours, but we did not hurry. We were enjoying ourselves. Late at night, with the music still roaring, we divided up our ammunition and people. Three *compañeros* stayed behind, with most of the bullets and the very best guns. The others left, climbing straight up the cliffs to an invisible ledge far above. Then our work was finished, and we sat down to wait for dawn, and the army.

We did not have to wait for very long. With the first rays of sunlight, we could see the lines of camouflaged soldiers far below, hurrying up the trails to find us and to kill us. They arrived in big trucks, waving guns and shouting to one another. We watched quietly as they wound their way upwards, higher and higher, closer and closer to the old fort. It took a long time, but finally they reached the single-file trails that drew towards the boulders where our *compas* lay in waiting. At first the soldiers were cautious, but after edging along slowly, and with no mishap, they grew impatient and began hurrying forward toward where all the noise and smoke had been the night before. Perhaps they thought we had all moved on, past the pile of rocks they were heading toward. Who knows what they thought. They hurried, throwing care aside, straight into the rifle fire of the three *compañeros* hidden in the trenches we had dug. Many of the soldiers fell immediately— there was no place to run or to take cover. Those who did not fall from the bullets slid over the edge trying to escape. After only a few minutes, this part of the battle was over, with heavy losses to the army, the soldiers running and falling in a desperate retreat.

The next phase of the battle was more difficult, but we were well prepared. The army came back up the mountainside again, very quickly and furiously indeed, but this time not with foot soldiers. This time they came with low flying helicopters. From far above, we could see the machine gun fire raking the old fort site, over and over again. The noise and smoke, it was terrible to watch. The helicopters also dropped mortars and even fire onto the rocks below. Finally, after what seemed like forever, the pilots flew off, evidently confident that no one could have survived such an attack. Once again, far below, we could see the foot soldiers climbing up the mountainside towards the fortress, this time more careless than ever. From the way they walked, so relaxed and carefree, you could see that they expected to find nothing but cadavers up there among the rocks.

But we had dug very deep and strong trenches, and the boulders had given much protection. The three *compañeros* were fine, and waiting for the soldiers to come back. Up above, we, too, were ready and waiting for combat. As the soldiers rounded the bend once again, the three *compañeros* opened fire from behind the rocks, and we climbed down from our ledge and ambushed the troops from the other side. We fought that day as we had never fought before. I felt inspired, wild. When my rifle jammed I found myself wanting to hurl it down below at the soldiers as if it were a club. We knew that victory was ours.

I had long ago ceased to believe in spirits, but I know that they were there with us. I could sense them, our ancestors, there in the shadows, fighting with their obsidian spears and feathered arrows, fighting for the survival of their very world. We were fighting together that day, against the same enemy and the same terrible fate. We were fighting together—to the last man, and to the last ancient rock.

PART III
The New
Generation

Note

The following stories describe the new conditions of the 1990s. The URNG, at the time of this writing, is at the negotiation table with the army and the government of Guatemala. Military generals, who long insisted the guerrillas had been virtually wiped out, now discuss the terms and conditions of potential peace plans with the leaders of the four revolutionary groups. Meanwhile, the guerrilla troops have become well-armed, well-trained and completely committed to seeing out the end of the war. They have come down from the volcanoes now, and march through the populated areas near the southern coast and close to the capital itself. For nearly five years, their voices have rung out twice a week in a short-wave radio broadcast that the army has been unable, with all its weaponry, to silence. Meanwhile, the ranks swell with the younger brothers and sisters of those who fell long before. Grandparents, having buried their children, now send their grandchildren to continue the battle for a free Guatemala. Refugees, growing old in exile, send their sons and daughters to fight in their place. Peace may be near or it may be far away. It does not matter for the people who have patience. They are willing to continue to struggle and to die until the curse of the last five hundred years is broken, and their people are free at last.

A Visit to Jennifer from Martina

I sat in my quiet office, staring dully at the telephone, trying to compose my scattered thoughts into a reasonable memorandum of law. I was back in the U.S.A., or, rather, halfway back. A big chunk of me never returned at all. A few too many photographs, a few too many people hidden once too often in my dingy hotel room—in the end no choices had been left for me. The menacing figures had followed me everywhere, watching, standing guard across the street, leaning forward to try and identify the faces of my friends. And so the time to leave had abruptly arrived, catching me off guard and resistant. I returned Christmas week to the chaos of radio commercials and jammed airports, back to my office where I had once felt happy and challenged by my work. But now I was only able to stare at the four walls during the day and stay late after closing time, exhausted and in tears. The *compas*, I knew, were still down there, fighting, hungry, determined, dying, and there was no longer anything I could do. It was over.

The telephone rang as I was staring at it, and over the wires floated the lilting voice of Martina, as if summoned by my suffering. I was frightened for a moment, disoriented, wondering if she was calling from Guatemala, wondering who was dead. But she was in the United States. On what papers and with what connections, I could not imagine, but I was not surprised, either. Martina can do these things.

She is a *compa*. Hearing her voice, I began to cry, happy to hear her, desperate to go back. She seemed to intuit my feelings and spoke soothingly for a few moments, bracing me. She told me she would only be in the States for a week or so, that would be enough sightseeing. She told me about shopping, about going to the movies, about the new foods she had been sampling. Then, in the familiar old codes she had used before with me, she told me that she was with another *compa*, that they would be leaving the U.S. together. Would I be at the airport in a certain city in case there was any problem with the authorities? We agreed quickly on the time and place, and I flew out the door to wire her extra cash and to buy her gifts she didn't need.

On the appointed day, I raced through the airport, ducking the luggage carts and mini-wagons carrying passengers to remote wings of the terminal. My arms were full of odds and ends: chocolates, some flowers, a book, a pink wool sweater in a size only North Americans could wear. My heart was pounding as I reached the small coffee shop. Martina was there, sitting cross-legged on the carpet. She looked very different. Her luxuriant hair was bound into two tight braids and looped out of sight at the nape of her neck. Her golden skin was wan, deprived of sunlight in our wintry climate. Dressed in a gray sweater and neatly pressed jeans, her slender figure seemed too frail, too short, to be an adult woman's. Her face was the same, though, pretty and soft only to those who looked no further. She stood up, smiling, to embrace me, and it was only then that I saw the child. He had been sitting on her lap, cuddled close in a wool blanket. As

The New Generation

Martina hugged me tightly, she explained that this was the other *compañero*. This was her son, Carlitos. She had come to take him home.

We had only one hour for talking. She told me quickly of the others. Christian was dead, Elena in hiding. The rest were still alive. Martina herself had gone into hiding briefly, but then gone back to work up in the jungles. She was staying out of the cities more and more now. It was on her last jungle tour that she had talked late into the night with an old friend, and together they had decided it was time for Carlitos to come home. She had sent him away, to safety with a Guatemalan family in exile in France. He had been barely over a year old then. She had not wanted him to die with her. She had wept, thinking she would never see his little face again, but she had saved his life. Her husband had already been killed. But now Carlitos was nearly six and her friend had reminded her that he must come home soon and take his place among his people before it was too late. He must learn his Mayan language; he must learn his ancestry. If necessary, he must learn to fight, as his own mother and father had fought, as so many others had fought. In the end, what use was triumph if the children were lost to their own people?

I watched Carlitos slurp happily at a milkshake while Martina told me her story. She could not take her eyes off her child, nor could I. He was dressed in a Mickey Mouse T-shirt and little-boy overalls with bright red sneakers on his tiny feet. His face was a neat replica of any Mayan carving. His face was Martina's face, full-lipped, sculpted, the eyes bright and black. He was at ease, holding her arm, talking

to us in French, a language his mother was still trying to learn. As I stared at him, he stared back, bold
and impudent and unafraid, just like his mother,
making me laugh out loud.

Martina told me proudly that he had chosen to
go home with her. She had seen him last when he
was not quite three, and then her situation had
grown too dangerous for travel. So now, several
years later, she had gone to see him with her heart
in her mouth, wondering if he would remember her,
wondering how she could win him back. The family
there had been very good to him, and they had loved
him as their own. But they had been good to her, as
well. Every day they had shown him her picture,
and told him that she was his mother, that she was
beautiful and brave, that she loved him, and that
someday soon, she would come to take him home
with her so that they could be together. Carlitos
waited patiently for that day, trusting her to return
for him. At first he was shy, but she did not push or
rush him. She just stayed close by for a few weeks
until he came to know her again, until he could
remember how she loved him. And finally, when she
asked if he would like to return home to Guatemala
with her, he had told her yes. As Martina told me
the story, her eyes sparkled with tears.

The loudspeaker blared out her flight number,
and we grabbed up her things and hurried towards
the gate. Carlitos ran to take her hand. He spoke to
her in French, and she answered in Mayan, and
somehow they understood each other perfectly. He
was happy and excited, pointing to the airplanes,
eager to fly, dancing up and down as she checked in
at the counter. His papers were false, but the flight

attendant did not look closely, and the moment of worry passed. And suddenly it was time for us to say good-bye. My head was spinning in jubilation and pain. I held Martina closely and kissed Carlitos. She would leave him with her mother and sisters; he would be safe enough. But I knew what she was going back to. There had been too many years for her, too many close calls, too many friends, now dead, who under torture must have identified her. How much longer could she last? Unbidden, the memory of that night in the hotel pushed its way into my mind, and I could see her there, at the balcony, defiant, demanding a razor, not taking her eyes from the darkened car below.

She touched my cheek, remembering, too, and then she was gone into the corridor, taking her beloved child with her. Tears began to stream down my face. "Martina!" I wanted to say, "Live ! Live!"

She had vanished too quickly. Needing one last look, I stepped over the ropes for a glimpse into the corridor. Martina glanced back and smiled. One braid had come loose, spilling her perfect hair across her back. With a cat-like movement, she swung Carlitos up onto her shoulders and turned to board the plane. A weary passenger paused, staring at her strange beauty, fumbling with his boarding pass. And then she was out of sight, hurrying off, back to the homeland her child must learn to love and to serve, back to her own valiant struggle and probable death.

Bernardo

It's all my little brother's fault. That rascal! Here I am thirty-six years old, huffing and puffing around the mountains with these kids, my old desk job and my favorite beer hall in some other world. What can I say? I am happy to be here, and I am certainly a lot healthier. My pot belly is gone, and I can't get hold of enough cigarettes to do me much harm. It is a hard life, but a good one. And it is the one I have chosen. I just have to laugh and shake my head sometimes, though, when I think about it all. You see, many years ago I had dropped out of the movement. Things were just too hard, too frightening. Then my little brother David got to me. I mean he really got to me with something he did one day, something that forced me to think. And so I ended up becoming reinvolved, and coming up here, years after I should have in the first place. If you think all this is a bit comical, I tell you—it's all his fault. If you ever see him, tell him I said so. And give him a very big hug from me. Damn if I don't miss that kid!

I started out as a young city intellectual, like so many of us. I was a student; I wanted to be an architect; I was involved in a lot of activities on campus. Activities like organizing demonstrations, attending political meetings. I did volunteer work with the city unions, signed petitions for land reform. All this must sound so tame to you, so ordinary, but you have to understand that in our country, such involvements can cost you your life. Thousands of us have died in very terrible ways for committing such small, tame acts.

The New Generation

For a long time, I felt certain that I was immortal. You know how young people can be. I never seemed to be noticed, never was followed, never was stopped or questioned. My phone never rang in the middle of the night, no mysterious voice ever promised me death or destruction. I felt certain that I had outsmarted everyone, and that for people like me there was no real risk. So I bounced happily from task to task and even began to mingle more with some friends in the city underground. They had not asked me to join them yet, only to run small errands. I didn't know for sure what my answer would be if they ever did ask, but I supposed it would be yes. I really wasn't thinking much about it one way or the other, and I am sure that's why they never tried to bring me in any deeper. A revolution is no game. This they knew, but I didn't.

Had things stayed quiet, I would probably have matured bit by bit, thought things through more and become a truly committed member of the underground back then. But there was never a chance for any slow maturation. Things changed so quickly, the city became such a hellish place. You know some of this history, I am sure. I am talking about the late 1970s and early '80s, those nightmare years. Even now they make me sick to remember. Those were the years when demonstrators for Indian rights were burned alive in the Spanish Embassy. Our people tried to march on May day, for better labor protections, and were murdered by the dozen, either on their way home from the demonstration or few days later. When I say murder, I am not talking about a simple bullet to the head.

Things were terrible. I walked out of my classroom one day and stood waiting for a bus at the campus parking lot. It was early evening and there were long lines of people waiting for rides. A mini-bus rolled up, and I remember stepping forward, hoping there would be a space for me. But as the side door opened, a masked man appeared and opened fire on us with his automatic rifle. I will always remember his voice, so choked with hate. As people fell, I could only turn and run.

I began to fear the campus I had once loved. I began to skip my classes and avoid meeting with my friends. One by one, the other members of the student union were disappearing, either attacked on campus and abducted in broad daylight or dragged from their beds in the middle of the night. For a while I went with the others to search the morgues, but after finding a few friends there, on those metal slabs, I didn't go any more. Such terrible deaths! There are some things it is better not to know.

I still lingered for a while, though, with some of the other groups in the city. I came now and then to the larger union meetings. Sometimes I still marched, though always with a big bag over my head, small holes punched out for the eyes. It was the bus riots that broke my heart and ended my activities once and for all. After that I could not go on at all, not with anything.

The riots had started with a big increase in the bus fares, approved by the government. The rich were unaffected, for they had their own cars. But things were already so hard for all of us poor people and this meant things would get even worse. Servants would have to walk the long distance from the *barrios* to the fancy houses of the rich in Zone

Twelve. The poor could not get their crops to market. Students, after long hours of work to pay their tuition, would be walking to night classes at the university. There were so many other things to tax, so many other luxuries to make more expensive. A price increase aimed directly at the poor, during a time of such terrible repression, struck us like a slap in the face. We were already filled with so much rage and impotence. And so we all took to the streets, to cry out against this squeezing of blood from a stone.

I was with a young woman, Ana Alicia, with whom I was very much enamored. She didn't know this, for I hadn't yet gathered the courage to tell her. She was so much braver than I was, still active, despite everything, and I admired her very much. She was gentle and very feminine, despite her strength. Not pretty really, but very soft, very serene. I remember especially her soft, round hands that I wanted so much to take in my own. But for her, I probably would have avoided the streets that day; but she was going, and so I went, too, just to be with her.

Things started out quietly enough, but there were so many of us, so very many, that I knew we would never make it through the afternoon. The army would never tolerate such a strong showing of public criticism. Ana Alicia and I were crowded to the side of a small square, listening to a masked speaker crying out through a bullhorn, the crowd roaring its reply. I was feeling frightened, waiting for the first blow to fall, when helicopters began circling overhead. I craned my neck to see down the nearby streets, a light sweat breaking out on my face. To my right, I could just glimpse them, the big police vans and the army jeeps, pulling over and parking a few blocks away. Armed and uniformed men were running towards us, silently, and in single file. I grabbed Ana Alicia by the arm and started pulling her away from the crowd, towards a small alley I knew of, where I hoped that we could hide, or at least get out of the way. Too late, though, it was much too late.

A scream of terror suddenly rose from the crowd as the armed men bore down on us all, clubbing us, beating us, lobbing tear gas into the center of the square. A policeman brought a baton down hard over the back of my head, almost knocking me out, but I managed to stay on my feet and start running with Ana Alicia. Everyone was running then, trying to break out of the square, but we were pretty well surrounded. I was choking on the tear gas and half-blinded with tears, but I remember Ana Alicia, in the midst of all this frenzy, calmly examining the back of my head and wrapping her scarf around the wound. I didn't know it then, but I was bleeding badly. I only remember those soft, steady hands and the sound of gunfire beginning, not far away.

We actually managed to get out of the square—I don't remember how. I only remember pushing and shoving and running, and the terror I felt. I had thought we were safe, and had slowed down to catch my breath, when it happened. We were rounding a corner on the way back to her apartment when four men leaped from behind a building and began to give us a terrible beating. They were not in uniform, but they had the clubs and guns that only soldiers and police can get hold of in our country. They were beating me badly, but for some reason they were focusing on Ana Alicia. Her, they were beating to kill. I don't know why, maybe she had been involved in more than I had known. They were cursing her and smashing their batons and rifle butts down on her tiny frame. Finally one of them held her head, while the other brought his weapon down across her face with all his strength. I remember that her eye was protruding and I remember trying to reach out for her hand. But that's all I remember. When I awoke in the street hours later, she was not there. I read in the newspaper that she had been killed in a car crash, but I did not attend her funeral. She was only one of many who had died, but she was the one I cared about.

I never attended anything again. No more meetings, no more marches. I left off my studies and never returned to the campus. My nerves were so terrible, I could not sleep, and for a long time I couldn't really work, either. My family was good to me. They asked no questions, taking care of me for many months until I was well enough to look for a job. I forgot about architecture and started a small business in sign painting and graphics. I drank too much and read too little. I never married. And so the years passed, one by one. And in my own way I was content. I was safe and took care never to look back.

And then came September, 1985. For years, the city had been quiet. It was as if the terror had finally won out against us all, driving us off the streets and back into our houses. We had been silenced. The only ones who still dared to protest were the people in GAM, looking for their vanished family members. And two of those leaders had ended up dead themselves that year. I had admired them from afar, almost despite myself, but I had never joined their marches, or spoken up in their defense. I was simply too afraid. It was hard enough just to survive from day to day. Our economy was collapsing rapidly, and I was trying to feed myself and my old parents, as well. It wasn't easy. And then the government, just like before, announced a bus fare increase—a big one. And once again, somehow, this hit a public nerve. Too many of us remembered.

My youngest brother, David, was only fourteen years old when all this started up again. He, too, remembered the old riots, but through the romantic eyes of a child. In a way he saw me as a hero of sorts, if he could only get me off my rump and dust me off a little. He began coming home from the good Catholic boys' school, where I was paying his tuition, telling me that the new bus fares were going to be passed, that something must be done. It was unfair to the poor, and it was also an insult to the memory of those who had died before, he said. The army had gone too far in their corrupt and cruel rule, and must be stopped. I would wince to hear these words, so much like my own, then calmly explain to him that nothing could be done. We would talk for hours, me becoming more and more frightened by his obstinacy, he more and more irritated by my cowardice. I fell back into my old, agitated insomnia, and David joined a student group and began to stay out late at night, despite my protests.

And then it started, the noise of a crowd surging past my office, the rhythmic chanting, the many feet. They were shouting "Join Us, Join Us!" and I found myself drawn to my window. Looking down at the street I saw a crowd, all right, but not the kind that I had expected. It was a crowd of children. Well, teenagers, David would hasten to correct me. But it was a crowd of terribly young adults. There was a small group at the head of the marchers, a gaggle of boys in blazers with blue bookbags in one hand, colorful banners waving proudly from the other. They were surrounded by a determined looking contingent of girls in parochial school kilts and knee socks, also carrying banners, shouting in turn through a bullhorn. Behind them came more and more students, mostly high-school age, some university, and behind them, a very cautious looking crowd of adults. For a while I stared in disbelief, and then, in a panic, wondered where David was. At that moment he burst through the door.

His hair was disheveled, but he still had his red school sweater on and his neat tan book bag in one hand. We began to talk at once, me begging him to stay out of it, screaming that a bus fare wasn't worth dying for, he begging me to join him, reminding me that the bus fare itself was only the tip of the iceberg. We are too much alike, David and I, and in the end we fought bitterly. I told him he was a damned fool. He told me that if I didn't have the balls to do something about our country, then he did. And with that he was out the door and into the street. I sat angrily at my desk for a while, cursing him, and then suddenly realized that he was gone and in terrible danger. And in a flash I knew how much I loved him.

I ran down the stairs two at a time and flung

myself into the street, running through the crowd, searching frantically for David. I ran past plaid kilts, blue book bags, and dark green soccer uniforms. I ran past team letters and parochial school insignias. I ran past dozens of slender, youthful figures, hearing their congratulations for my courage in joining them, caring only about one slight boy in a dark red sweater.

I found him, of course. There he was, right up front on the steps of the National Palace with another group of students. By now a huge crowd had gathered: women from the market place, businessmen, taxi drivers. Far down the street, too, I could see the police vans coming. I elbowed my way towards the front of the crowd, and finally found a place to stand where I could see, behind a wood fence where some construction workers had been tearing up the sidewalk. They were all huddled behind the fence, too, standing there in their hard hats, amazed, curious, and frightened. Behind us, on the commercial avenue, I could hear the metal shop shutters clanging down in anticipation of the uproar to come.

As I leaned over the top of the fence, straining, I saw David and the others, under the archways of the government offices, raise their fists slowly and solemnly, and then begin to sing. For a moment I could not hear the melody, but then the crowd hushed, and I could hear them very plainly. Fists raised, they were singing the national anthem. As I listened, I cannot tell you what I felt, it was too complex. It chokes me even now to remember that moment. As I turned to the construction workers next to me, I saw that they, too, were weeping, just as I was.

Well, David and I survived that day, I with terror, he with exhilaration. He is safe, now, because he was very lucky—I was able to get hold of a car through a friend and bundle him out of the city just a few hours before the police got to our house. He is somewhere else now, working and happy. I returned to the city and reconnected with an old friend. Right away, he put me to work with the underground. I can't tell you why, but my fears had suddenly disappeared. It's not that I didn't care any more; I certainly still wanted to live. It's just that somehow it had become so clear to me, how much it was worth whatever happened. I wanted to fight instead of forget. It was as if I had been, for years, anaesthetized. But no longer.

After awhile, it became unsafe for me in the city, so I chose to come up here, to the mountains, and make a fool of myself trying to keep up with these younger *compañeros*. I wasn't interested in running away any more, in looking for asylum in some country that could never understand me. It is difficult here, but it is good. I want to see the triumph. It is so close, but I can accept death now. Only God is immortal. I want to die with my boots on.

The Baby Tiger
and Jorge Medico

You would think, after the Commando Squirrel, that we would have learned our lesson about wild animals and pets. But we didn't, or at least I didn't. I still missed Sisifu, no matter how wicked he had been, and I still had fantasies about someday having a house with dogs and cats and horses and parrots and fish. I am just the kind of person that needs to have animal friends around, or life isn't quite right.

It wasn't very long before I had another chance at a pet. After all, we live up here in the mountains, where there are plenty of animals. It's just hard to catch them when they're young enough to tame. But this time I found a new born tiger. Not the kind of tiger they have in Africa, this would have been too much pet even for me. But it was a baby tigrillo, the kind that grows to be only as high as this table here, but has the same beautiful fur. It was right after a very bad series of bombings by the army that I found the baby. I guess the mother had been frightened off by the explosions, because she was nowhere to be found. Even when I picked up the cub and it began to mew in fear, she did not reappear.

It was a tiny male baby, his eyes still sealed tightly shut, his little arms and legs so soft and defenseless. When I put him down, he would try to walk, but really couldn't manage. He couldn't have been much more than a day old, and was obviously going to die if someone didn't help him out. Of course, this was as much of an excuse as I needed. Who could expect me to leave a poor little newborn to die? After all, he had been abandoned because of our war, not his. And so I placed him gently in my shirt pocket and carried him up to the camp to the kitchen fire.

Naturally, the little creature immediately became the center of attention. I am not the only one with a soft spot for animals, let me tell you, and I knew I would have plenty of supporters for keeping the baby with us. And sure enough, I did. The other *compañeros* came running from all over the camp to see the tigrillo, admire his perfectly striped fur, and touch his tiny little paws. Even the sentry came down and got in a few minutes of admiration before being ordered back to his post. There was much cooing and singing to the little one and vying for his attention, and I felt like a proud parent showing off a child. After a while we spread down an old rag in front of the fire, and nestled the tigrillo into its folds. He promptly yawned and fell sound asleep, in a little mound of soft fur.

While he slept we all got into an argument about what he should be named. Everyone had a different idea, and each suggestion had to be given very serious consideration. After all, it was a serious decision. In the end, we reached no agreement, and for the time being, began calling him Tigrillo, which was appropriate enough. It was while we were talking that I realized that an even more important matter was at hand, namely, what to feed him, and how. He was far too young to eat real food, this much I knew. He would need to have milk. And so

221

we ran off to Abram's tent and badgered him into a small ration of powdered milk for the new baby. Then we boiled up some water, and dinner was ready, just as Tigrillo began to wake up and mew.

Feeding him presented still more problems. He was too little to figure out how to lap the milk up from a small plate, and he choked when we tried to pour it into his mouth from a spoon. It was really heartbreaking to watch him trying to eat, waving his little paws around in search of his mother's body. So I went up to Jorge Medico's tent. I knew he was away caring for some people who had been wounded over on the far slopes. But I also knew he would forgive me. Jorge always forgives everything. So I took the eyedropper out of his eyedrop bottle and covered the bottle back up with a tight plastic wrap. Then I returned to the fire and fed the baby through the dropper, one drop at a time. This technique worked, and for the rest of the night we took turns holding him and feeding him droplets of milk. He was so popular that I had to get really tough about people overfeeding him and not letting him sleep enough. But I was also pleased to see that he was so appreciated.

When Jorge came back, sure enough, he forgave me the eyedropper theft, and even came down to the fire to play with the tigrillo and give him a checkup. He pronounced the baby to be in good health, even though he had been separated from his mother so early. And for the first week or so, Tigrillo really flourished. His eyes opened, and he was growing in leaps and bounds. Every single development was noted eagerly by the whole camp. So you can imagine how pleased we all were when the baby tried walking in earnest. Until then, he would try, but could only stagger a few steps before he fell flat. But now his legs were steadier. The problem was, he was still pretty weak, and since we had fed him so much, he was awfully fat for his little tiny muscles. So there came a very tragic day when a big mouse sneaked into the camp at night and bit the poor little thing. I heard Tigrillo's howl all the way back at my tent, and came running as fast as I could, as did everybody else. You would have thought we were being called to our positions during a surprise attack. We couldn't have run any faster. By the time we got there, though, poor little Tigrillo had staggered away from the mouse and collapsed at the edge of the fire, burning a little paw and singeing off his whiskers. Naturally we were beside ourselves and ran straight to Jorge Medico, dragging him from his bed, even though he'd just got back from another emergency. Good natured as ever, he came down and bound up the burned paw and comforted Tigrillo back to sleep.

The very next morning we called an emergency session of the Tigrillo protectors. We needed to figure out what to do, so that this wouldn't happen again. I wanted to take Tigrillo to sleep with me, and pretty much everyone agreed. But we also thought Tigrillo needed more muscle to support his weight. Maybe it was time to move him on to better food. And so we coaxed some Cerelac away from a *compa* who had recently been down to the villages, and fed it to the cub. He seemed to like it. After all, it was baby cereal, and what was good for human babies should be good for tiger babies, we reasoned. And it should give him the better nutrition he seemed to

223

need.

And for a few days, Tigrillo did fine on his new diet. He really seemed to be thriving. In the end though, he was just too young to eat all that we were feeding him, and the poor little thing ended up with a terrible case of diarrhea. His system just couldn't handle it. I wasn't really worried at first, and just fed him a little boiled water with a dash of salt and sugar to fight off dehydration. He was too tiny, though, and by early morning I became really frightened. So I took him back to the fire in the kitchen, wrapped him up in a blanket, then raced off once again, to rouse Jorge out of a sound sleep. As soon as he understood that the tigrillo was in danger, he jumped right out of bed and ran with me to the fire, just as if I had called him to the aid of a wounded *compañero*. He really understood how much this baby meant to us. He examined Tigrillo for a few moments and looked worried. The little cub was very weak and dehydrated already. But Jorge tended him carefully, shaving off the fur on his front leg, and hitching Tigrillo up to an I-V. Then he covered him back up and told us to keep him warm and let him rest.

For two days, we all kept turns sitting by the fire and keeping watch over the baby tiger. But we couldn't save him. Not even Jorge, with all his care and kindness could save him. The little creature had just been separated from his mother too soon. When he finally died, we all wept and were very unhappy. Then I wrapped Tigrillo up in his blanket and carried him out of the camp and gave him a decent burial, over there, on the back of that slope. I sat with him for a little while then, and remembered all the fun we'd had together. It was my way of say-ing good-bye. Then I went back to Jorge's tent, because I knew he wouldn't laugh at me for being so depressed over an animal. Jorge understands that I am just that way about creatures. I love them.

Jorge was there waiting for me. He had dug out his secret stash of cigarettes for me. Not that he smokes, but he knows most of the rest of us do, so he keeps a little supply ready for times like these. So we sat for a while and talked about Tigrillo, and about life in the mountains. I smoked up a storm and he even found some foil-wrapped candies. He has been up here for nearly twelve long years now, this wonderful man. He came up here on the run after his wife was murdered in the city, leaving behind a tiny child of his own that he never saw again. Life has not been easy to Jorge. Perhaps that is why he showers so much love on all of us. It is as if all of us together, as a big family, have taken the place of the wife and child he lost.

I knew Jorge understood me that night because he even began to play his classical music for me. He loves that music, Bach and Mozart and Handel. Me, I am more the rock-and-roll and salsa type of per-son, but I have to admit that his music was just right for that evening. I could just close my eyes and listen, and I felt strengthened, calmed. Perhaps, when I was in school, I should have listened to this old music much more seriously. That night, as I lis-tened, I suddenly understood Jorge better, too. He never does anything without his music. I remember once, during a very terrible period of combat last year, helping him to tend the wounded. They were all laid out in a row on the ground, and he was flying from one *compa* to the next, trying to keep them all alive. I was very worried about him, because he had not slept for days, and looked half-dead himself. There was not time to talk to him, though, we were both too busy applying tourniquets and stopping the blood. Then the others carried in Guillermo, who was so very young, and for me almost like a son. I had trained him myself and the sight of him stopped me in my tracks. He had been hit with a mortar, and even as I reached out to him, his eyes dimmed, and I knew he was dead. I looked up, weeping, for Jorge and saw him running towards me, through the smoke and the awful noise of the explosions. His headphones were around his neck, the wild and magical chords of the *Messiah* floating upwards to the sky above.

Diego and
La Voz Popular

It is all so different now. There have been so many changes. For an old timer like me, it is sometimes hard to believe. We eat well now. There are few luxuries but we are no longer hungry. I no longer crave a cigarette at night to mask the pain of emptiness in the pit of my stomach. There is enough to go around. We have boots and blankets, good backpacks, and sturdy utensils. There are books, a generator, even a small television to watch when we have the extra fuel. From time to time we can watch the newscasts, a soccer game, even a bit of a movie, although we always risk missing the ending scenes for lack of fuel. Even so, it does us good, that brief contact with the outside world. We have medicines and a fine doctor. We have secure evacuation routes for those too seriously wounded to be treated here. We have guns that shoot straight, supplies of ammunition, even mortars. Really, what more could we want, besides, of course, peace itself? It is truly hard for me to believe it all. We are the same people, fighting for the same cause. But it is a very different war. Thank God, it is a very different war.

Have you been listening to our radio program, "La Voz Popular"? When we first started broadcasting, the army was all over us, sending their best troops and their favorite bombs to wipe us out. The program was such a slap in the face to them that they could not allow us to continue. They could not let our voices reach the villagers. There were some difficult times for awhile, some heavy battles, and we lost several very special *compañeros*. To this day, it hurts me to think about their deaths. But the army was never able to take our volcano or stop our broadcasts. Ultimately, they took far more losses than we did. As you see, they do not come up here any more. They do not even try. We are in our fifth year now of "La Voz Popular." Can you understand what it means to us, to hear our own people speaking out over the airwaves? It is like watching our banner rise high above the mountains. After so many years of being hunted down and silenced, we are now heard.

It was not easy, setting up the radio station. There were so many problems involved: how to work out the power supply, how to get the equipment up here. Really, it all started with our engineering team. They dreamed up the whole scheme. I was sent down out of the mountains to study with them, to learn about the different mechanical parts, and practice making everything work. When I first started, I thought it was all crazy, very impractical. Of course, I loved the idea, but deep down inside I believed that only an engineer could come up with something that crazy. I used to tease them about it, asking them when we would be getting our underwater helicopters or our flying tanks. As you can see, they had the last laugh. Everything has worked out just as they planned.

It took months for me to learn everything, but I enjoyed my new studies and was fascinated with all the new equipment. I went over it piece by piece, nut by bolt, wire by wire, with Estuardo. He is a very brilliant man but also very patient and humble—the kind of *compa* who likes you to know everything that he does. We worked together every day. I would say he taught me everything, but he would never permit those words. To him, the hours we spent together were hours of sharing. Nothing more and nothing less.

And so my time in our underground house passed quickly. I was reading and practicing, learning about sound waves and electricity. I could not go out much, but I didn't mind. Most of the last decade I have lived out-of-doors, without a roof over my head, so the change was good for me. There was a puppy in the courtyard, and a soccer ball. When I wasn't working or studying, I was enjoying the good food, playing soccer with the others, or trying to teach the puppy some tricks. I have always wanted a puppy in the mountains, but felt that the barking could endanger us. My *compañera* has one now, though. Have you seen it? She brought one home, and I'll be damned if she didn't train him to keep quiet. He never barks at all, even though you can tell how much he wants to. I'll never figure out how she did that.

When the time came to go, Estuardo helped me pack up the most important piece of the new radio equipment because it would be my responsibility to carry it back up into the volcanoes. It was heavy, but I was strong, and he knew I would take very good care of it. He wrapped it up like a mother bundling a child against the cold, reminding me how delicate it was, how gently it must be treated, and how it should never be allowed to get wet, under any circumstances. All this I knew, of course, but I reassured him that I would give it careful pro-

229

tection indeed. Then we wished each other luck, and embraced, both very excited about the new project we were about to launch. What a wonderful dream it was back then, to think of our voices finally reaching down, out of the volcanoes. I was both thrilled and moved, and felt very honored to be able to participate.

Getting me from the house back to the base in the mountains was no simple task. The army, of course, patrols those areas heavily, looking for people just like me. The plans had been prepared with great care and detail. Before I knew it, I was running up the steep slopes of a cornfield with my heavy backpack. It was dark out as I hiked swiftly up the trails for most of the night, eager to place as much distance as possible between myself and the patrolled areas before dawn. Around two in the morning, I rested a bit, drinking some water mixed with dried milk and gobbling down some cold rice. I didn't stop for long, though, and dared not build a fire. In the town, I had rested well and even put on a bit of weight, so I had plenty of energy for the climb. By dawn I reached the top of a ledge quite close to our encampment, and for the first time in twenty-four hours I felt that I, and the radio unit, were safe from harm.

There was a small spring in the clearing where I had stopped. Suddenly I felt very tired and thirsty. I unstrapped my pack, placing it firmly on the ground, and knelt down by the cool water to drink and wash my face. Then I sat on a large rock to chew a bit more rice and rest a few moments. There was not far to go; I knew I would make it to the encampment by mid-morning. Like they say, so near and yet so far. As I sat there, rubbing my shoulders, I heard a strange creaking, almost groaning sound that I could not recognize. When I looked up, I saw my backpack sliding ever so gradually towards the edge of the steep cliffside I had just climbed. It was the rainy season, and the muddy earth was giving way under the dense weight of the radio as it inched toward the edge, and its doom.

I swear to you I have never, absolutely never, moved so fast in all my life. I sprang off my rock as if it were a hot coal, and dashed frantically to the top of the ledge. For a moment I thought all was well, for my fingers were within inches of the pack. But just as I reached out to grab it, it tipped back and tossed itself right over the edge. I was left standing at the top of the cliff, my mouth a big, round, horrified "O." I could see it tumbling down through the rocks. Every time it hit the ground there was a terrible crashing sound. Even after it was out of sight, I could still hear it. Crash! Crash! Crash! I could hear it all the way down. With every crash, my heart went Boom! Boom! Boom! as if to keep it company. Then there was an appalling silence.

For a while, I just stood there, too shocked to do anything but stare down the mountainside. What was I going to do? What could anybody do, at that point? How would I ever explain to Estuardo? Finally, I started wandering back down the trail, determined to recover the pieces, at least. All the way down, there were signs of the devastation, big holes in the ground where the radio bored in on impact, a group of trees with their tops sheared off. It was not a pretty sight at all. But I kept on going, following the crash marks, until I found the pack, sunk down deep in the mud. It took me a while to excavate it, but I did, and then opened up the flaps and pulled out the radio.

Miraculously, it was still in one piece. Nothing had broken off, nothing seemed bent or twisted. I opened it up, and everything seemed to be in order. I knew, deep inside, that it would never function again, but I needed to have hope. So I dusted it off and placed it gently on a flat rock in the sun. Then I pulled out my notebook and began running some of the tests I had learned to perform. To my great amazement, the little lights blinked on and off. I tested some more and found that all of the circuits worked just fine. The radio was functioning as if nothing had ever happened. I will never understand this. Perhaps it struck only soft mud instead of rocks on the way down. Perhaps its heavy metal casing shielded it from the impact. None of us has ever been able to explain it. All I can say is, it certainly is a good piece of equipment.

And so we have our "Voz Popular" broadcasts twice a week. The crazy idea worked perfectly, and the fragile machinery turned out to be, quite literally, indestructible. I have learned up here that you have to have a lot of faith and a lot of patience. All in good time, things will be resolved. I think about these things when I hear about the peace talks. There was a time when I would never have believed that the army would recognize us or sit down at the table with our leaders, let alone make any genuine concessions. For so long, they were bent on our extermination as the only acceptable conclusion. And yet now they are negotiating, conversing, listening to what our people have to say. Who knows when peace will come? It may be far off still, but suddenly it is a possibility, very much within our reach. Some day we will be able to lay down these weapons for once and for all. When the war is over, that is when our real work will begin. There will be so much building to do. Our people need health services, new roads, electricity, better food supplies, cooperatives, farm machinery. So many things we will need to work on, to put together, to provide. How I look forward to it all. My faith is very strong.

The Volcano,
as Told by Jennifer

It's true what they say. You can't go home again. I tried for a long time, but it never quite worked out. After I saw Martina off, I realized that it never would. Like Pandora's box, my mind had been opened, and could not be resealed. The Guatemalans could no longer be relegated to the half-world of frightening television images or stark statistics. Now they were real people, friends. Yet there was no going back to my old life in Guatemala, either. My days there had ended badly, and my return would only cost Guatemalan lives. The time had come to find some other way.

It took a while, but I did find a way to return, at least temporarily. And so, after long and careful negotiations, I found myself hidden away in a small room with a dark-haired *compañera* named Eliza. A short, wiry woman, she helped me comb through the contents of my backpack, telling me what was missing, such as extra batteries, and what was excess weight, such as two spare shirts. I would only need one. The plaid would have to go—it was too bright, anyway. She checked my small cooking pan, noting the flimsy handle, but nodded her approval at the heavy socks and lightweight blanket. We bartered for a while over the need for my five pads of paper and the thick bundle of pens. But I held my ground on these since they were for my book, and finally, she relented. Then we practiced the code words that I would be using the following morning, switching roles until I had both sides of the conversation memorized. You must always know the other person's lines as well as your own, she explained. Otherwise you could be tricked and fall captive to the army, a most inconvenient event. Eventually, even she was convinced that I was well rehearsed, and together we went out into the quiet streets for dinner and a movie. There was only one theater in town and the only film showing was *Rambo*, but we didn't mind. We sat in the back row, arm-in-arm, giggling and munching popcorn like two school girls. Our work complete, we knew that it was time to play. Tomorrow would be full enough.

Back at the hotel we took turns taking hot showers. Then Eliza told me stories for a while: stories from her village about women with magical powers, love stories about star-crossed young people, stories of mythical jaguars and birds. I listened contentedly and then fell asleep easily on my small cot, mesmerized by her soft voice. I felt quite serene, for somehow Eliza made everything seem very normal, even ordinary. I slept soundly through the night, awakening at dawn to quiet melodies from a classical music station. No jolting alarm clocks for Eliza. As I struggled into my lace-up boots and sturdy clothing, she brought a steaming breakfast tray: rich coffee, baked plantains, and corn tortillas stuffed with black beans—my favorite foods. (She had asked me earlier what they were and had somehow found a way to prepare them). We ate together for the last time, urging food on one other. I hoped silently that we would see each other again, someday, but knew it would be unlikely. I didn't even know her real name and probably never would.

BRIDGE OF COURAGE

A horn honked downstairs, and we embraced quickly. She did not accompany me to the street—there was no need for her to see the driver's face. Instead she wished me well, and closed the door gently behind me. As I descended, I could hear her firmly turning the key in the lock. The sound made me uneasy, and for the first time I felt frightened. Perhaps, really, I was not cut out for all this. My throat felt tight and dry, but then I thought of how badly I had wanted to go back, how long I had pleaded for this chance. It was either this, or my old office in the States. The image of my waiting desk braced me, and I shouldered the pack and skipped on down the remaining stairs, determined.

By nightfall I was running. There was enough of a moon that I could see where I was going, but it didn't really help much. We were in a thick forest. My feet were clumsy in their heavy boots, making me stumble over the twisting roots and shifting rocks. The soft earth, soaked through with the heavy rains, slid out from under me with every step. There were five *compañeros* running at my side, dressed in olive green and well-armed. They encouraged me in low voices, warning me of unsteady ground or sudden drops. Although I could not see their faces in the dim light, I could recognize their accents, the soft, bird-like tones of the Mayan highlanders, and the sound made me feel at ease, at home. They helped me across the rivers, giggling as I teetered back and forth on the slippery rocks, hugging me when I reached the other side in safety. My well-being was definitely a community affair, to be discussed together as we ran across the cornfields and up the narrow trails. Was I thirsty? Did I need rest? Were my boots adequate for the muddy slopes of the volcano?

We ran for hours, the trails becoming fainter and steeper with every step. After a while, we were climbing, and I found myself reaching forward to clutch at vines and rocks, pulling myself up and forward. The *compañeros* grew more relaxed as we moved higher, reassuring me that we had long since left army territory. Our pace slowed, but we continued upwards, distancing ourselves as much as possible from the danger. To my amazement, I was not even tired—the exhilaration of the return filled me with energy I normally did not have. The volcano, even in the semi-darkness was beautiful, the steep cliffs above us etched sharply against the night sky.

At three or so in the morning, we stopped and set up camp, the *compas* swiftly unpacking heavy tarpaulins and spreading them on the ground. The one named Daniel took charge of nourishment, disappearing in the direction of a bubbling stream and returning with a delicious drink of cold, sweetened milk. They drank it down swiftly, offering me the greatest share, then spoke quietly about the next few hours: who would stand post, who would gather roots for a morning meal, who would find the wood and build the morning fire. Then they pulled out their blankets and piled them up in an overlapping heap. We slept together like that, all in a row on the tarpaulins, curled up side by side under the shared covers. The next thing I knew it was morning.

I awoke with the dim light of a rising sun filtering down through the trees. Daniel was already up and silently preparing a small fire, kneeling down on large rubbery leaves to keep the mud off his tidy uniform. Abram was nearby, scraping and slicing some tuberous roots into a small black cooking pot. In the light, I could see their faces for the first time, Daniel with the sweet, open expression of a villager, Abram looking steady, thoughtful. He was older than the others, perhaps my own age, in fact, and had the sturdy body of a laborer. Eloy I could not see, for he was on the ledge above us, sending a radio message back to the base camp. Antonio and Carlos lay on either side of me, sound asleep. Looking down at them, I could see that they were very young, perhaps not quite twenty. Their faces were round and rosy, their closed eyes ringed with long black lashes. Antonio, to my amusement, showed the deep dimples of a child. Dressed in their uniforms, their boots still on their feet, they were sleeping soundly, their rifles only inches from their fingertips.

Dora

No, no my friend, you must not idealize us. We are happy that you have so much affection for us, and that you respect us, but we have plenty of faults. We are very human. We bicker with each other all the time, just like little children, and we complain all the time, too. Maybe we've just been too shy to be cry babies right in front of you. Take me, for example. I can really snarl when my knee starts acting up. I just have to be careful not to say anything about it to the medic, or he would send me down out of the mountains. That would be really terrible, since this is my home now. But believe me, I can really complain up a storm when he's not around. And you should have heard us all back when that damned squirrel was eating all of our food. For weeks, all you could hear at the camp was our cursing.

Jealousy is a good example, too. We are all terribly jealous when it comes to our relationships. I mean really, terribly jealous. It's just that none of us wants to admit this, because we know it is wrong, and foolish. In the first place, people are not property. In the second place, of course, a relationship should be built on trust. Also, we should trust our fellow *compañeros.* And we do, really. It's just that jealousy is not a rational thing. It just sneaks up on you, no matter how you try to fight it. It sneaks up on you, and you end up really making a fool out of yourself. Then everyone else teases you about it for awhile, even though secretly they understand, because they are the same way themselves.

I have been Roberto's *compañera* for many years, and I trust him and love him completely. The man is so patient and kindly, so responsible. He is much more than I deserve, really. And we have always been very happy. Yet I remember once coming back to our tent in the evening, and seeing him standing inside with Clarissa, a very shy young Mayan woman who had recently joined us. Clarissa was like a little sister to us both. Roberto had been assigned to teach her to read, and I had taken a special liking to her because of her good nature and her crazy laugh. I don't know what came over me, but I had a very nasty taste come into my mouth when I saw her standing there with Roberto. I knew perfectly well that nothing was going on, but I got this ugly feeling all the same. I tried to choke it back, but it was hard to hide. Clarissa slipped away after a few moments, and Roberto made fun of me for the rest of the night. I was really ashamed of myself, and I knew it was wrong, but I stayed grouchy for quite a while. Roberto understood. He is the same way. We are all the same way. We just can't help it.

Haven't you noticed how we are around the campfire at night? We are all such terrible flirts, too, even though we are careful not to cross the limits between flirting and something else. But sometimes we play right up to the edge, because let's face it, flirting is a lot of fun. There at the fire, Sonya will put her arm around Beto's shoulder, just an innocent little squeeze of course, and that will make Marcos squirm a little, since he likes her, too. Then Marcos will start combing my hair and Roberto will go off to wash the dishes so I can't see his face. The little one, Sara, will let Adam pull the handkerchief out of her pants pocket with his teeth, even though he is twenty years older than she is. And I noticed David edging up to you, don't deny it, even though he's twenty years younger.

When we hold dances up here, it's a free-for-all; everyone flirts with everyone. There's an unspoken rule that this is okay. And I'm sure you noticed what a great hula Sara can do even when she has a machete strapped to her back. I love to dance up here, even though the conditions are tough. You can put your rifle down, of course, but your boots have to stay on, and your cartridge belt, and the machete sling is attached to that so it's a little clumsy. All the same it's fun, as long as the ground isn't too slippery. On a good night we play the Beatles, and the *compañeros* who don't have a partner clap their hands up and down over their flashlights to give us a strobe light of sorts. Disco, heavens no, but fun, yes.

Really, all of us flirt, and all of us are jealous. Because we all know this, it doesn't create any real problems. This is just how we are. Why even Marisa, the *compañera* of the *comandante*, flirts. The *comandante* doesn't like this one bit either. When she gets really sassy he looks like he just bit into a hot chile pepper, but he can't say anything. After all, he is the *comandante*, so he has to set us a good example.

Laura

Will you keep my underpants while I'm away in combat? I'll only be gone a few days. They're my best pair, but they aren't quite dry yet, and I don't want them to blow away in the wind. I only have two other pairs. Here, have some of this corn drink, too, I made it myself this morning, but now it's time to wash up and get going. Come on, drink it down now. Good, isn't it? So how are your knees doing? Better, I hope. It's a long climb up here, I know. My first time up here was really hard, I remember. I cried a lot, believe me. Will you keep my extra shirt, too? And these chile peppers? A villager gave them to me last week, and they really taste great in the rice at night. You can eat one if you want. Just keep them separate from my underpants, okay? I don't want my underpants to smell like chiles.

Here, help me take down the tent strings. You're so much taller than I am. Your feet are so big, too. Don't take offense; you know I think you're very pretty. I would like to be taller, too, but I guess I'm not going to grow any more than this, 'cause I'm seventeen now. Can you reach that knot up there for me? I came up here when I was sixteen, even though my parents didn't want me to. In a lot of ways I suppose they were right. I really was imma-ture. But I've changed a lot up here. I am glad I came.

I grew up not far from here, did you know that? I was born in a small village, and my poor mother died a few days later. There was no money, so no medicine. I never knew her. I was raised by her servant, who loved me and decided to keep me with her and her family. She is the one I think of as my real mother, the one who cared for me and taught me everything I know. Later she had two sons of her own, my little brothers, Angel and Nery, and the three of us grew up together. In that family, I was never an outsider. And I was never treated as a lesser person because I was a woman. You see, my mother and father were both *compañeros*, so they had very different ideas about these things. They raised me to know my responsibilities to our people.

We had to leave Guatemala when I was about eight. It was during the time of the massacres, when the army was everywhere. I remember the helicopters and the soldiers, the shouts and the bad words, and my mother pulling me into the house, keeping me and my little brothers quiet in the shadows with bits of food. Sometimes at night I would wake up to find my parents talking softly in the darkness to someone I did not know. Other times I would awake to screams and fires in the distance. I didn't know what was going on, but I knew it was a time of fear.

Finally they came for my father. He had gone off to work in a distant corn field that day, and the soldiers had come to sweep through the area to find him and kill him. It was my old godmother who came running down the mountainside to warn us, to get us into hiding, before they came for us, as well. My mother didn't even stop to pack. She took nothing but her children. I remember our escape, but through the eyes of a child, with the images incomplete and fragmented. I remember the cold, and wanting more food, and being fascinated with the bright electrical lights of the towns we could see far below us. I cried, wanting my father, not thinking how my mother must have wanted to cry, too. Now, when Rafael is away at combat for a long time, and I worry, I remember my mother on that long trip.

We travelled slowly, hiding during the days, and at night walking and walking across endless fields and remote trails. There were strangers who appeared to guide us, who stopped us at the edge of each new village to give us new instructions and signal us to safety past their fields. If the army was nearby, they would take us to another place and bring us food. I know now what terrible risks these people were taking to help us reach safety, and I know now that they must have been *compañeros*. I like to think that someday, I will be able to find them again, with my mother, and thank them if they are still alive. Because we did reach Belize safely. And so did my father.

My parents could not bear to live far from Guatemala, and we stayed near the border. So for many years we hid and moved, and moved again, from village to village. My mother cut her hair and wore cheap cotton dresses, and we learned to speak like Belizeans. And that's how I still speak. You've heard the *compas* at night, at the campfire, start laughing at an expression I use, or the way I pronounce a word. Well, that's why. At least, here I am with friends, people who care for me. In Belize we were illegals, being hunted by the local police and also by roving Guatemalans who crossed the border to kill people like us. My mother's closest friend was murdered in this way. So we had to learn to act, and talk, and dress like Belizeans. And we did. After a while, my father managed to get false papers for us, and we were able to settle down and find work. That's when my parents sent me to public school, with the other children.

I loved school, and I became just like all the other teenagers. I liked dresses and lipstick, and I loved to flirt with all the boys. Sometimes I went to movies on the weekends with my girlfriends. I loved being pretty. My parents were flexible with me; they wanted me to be happy. But they never let me forget who we were. Every night when my brothers and I returned from school, my mother and father would sit down with us and we would all talk together. We would talk about Guatemala, what was happening there, what the people were suffering, why there was a revolution. We talked about the Mayan heritage of our country, the poverty, the goals of the *compañeros*. And we remembered together why we had fought, and why we had fled, and why, in whatever small ways possible, we must continue to contribute to the struggle of our people.

When I was sixteen, the *compañeros* came to my parents' house. They were returning from exile and stopped for food and a safe place to rest. At night my parents lit a small kerosene lamp and talked at the table with them until very late, hearing the news, staying in contact, keeping their hopes alive. Since I was old enough, I sat up with them. And it was on that night that I decided to go back to Guatemala and fight. My parents were not surprised; they had raised me for this decision. But they knew how young I was, and that I was upset about my boyfriend leaving me that week for another girl. They tried to convince me to wait another year, to finish school. My father even offered to go in my place, but everyone knew his knees would not last a week. He is too old now. And I was determined to go, so my parents and brothers held me close for a long time and then told me goodbye.

I really was too immature, I guess. A lot of *compañeras* come up here at sixteen, and they do just fine. But I cried all the time. I was homesick, first of all. And I just couldn't keep up. You see what short legs I have, no? It was very hard for me to learn to climb up and down the volcanoes all day. I didn't grow up in a mountain village like so many of the *compas*, and I wasn't in as good condition. In the beginning, I carried only a very small pack, but even that was hard for me. So I would fall behind, and sit down, and get cold and lonely and start to cry. And one of the *compas* would always come back for me, to wait with me, and rub my shoulders, and tell me encouraging words. They all knew I had to get through this, and remembered how it had been for them, too, at the beginning. So they would help me out with funny stories and give me extra food, and help pull me up the steepest ledges. And little by little I grew stronger, and stopped crying. I even became a good combatant.

I was hurt not long ago, in an accident. Did you hear about it? That's how Carlos lost the three fingers, too. We were practicing with grenades, over there at the other encampment, and one of them was defective. It exploded in Carlos' hand as soon as he pulled the pin, and it blew off his fingers. David took a big piece of shrapnel in the abdomen, and I caught a little one above the waist. Here, I'll show you the scar, see? I wasn't badly hurt. It was David who nearly died. Jorge, the medic, had to do full emergency surgery there in the tent to save his life, the hemorrhaging was so bad. I didn't feel much—it half knocked me out. I just remember the noise and the smoke, and Jorge's frantic face leaning over me. When I saw Jorge, I knew I would be fine. He just won't let us die, not him. And I was fine in a jiffy. That was just three months ago, and now there's nothing left but this little scar.

But I'll tell you a secret now; I know I can trust you. Ever since that accident, I've been afraid. Not of combat—I'm going to combat right now, and I'm not even nervous. The bullets don't frighten me at all, although they used to. It's the sound of the explosions that terrify me. They can be close by, or even really far away, and I start feeling nauseated and almost like I'm going to faint. Did you hear the mortars last night, in the distance? No? You see, you didn't even wake up, but I lay there, with my heart pounding, for the rest of the night. There's something about the sound, now. It terrifies me. You tell me it is normal and that it will pass. Rafael holds me at night and tells me the same thing. And I trust him completely, he's been up here so long. But three months? Isn't this a very long time for fear?

So I wrote to my mother in Belize, and told her everything. I told her there were times when I felt really close to despair, and that sometimes I thought about coming home, that maybe I was really too immature for the mountains that, perhaps, I should never have left home. I really opened up my heart to her, Jennifer. I was so depressed that day,

247

and really wished I could talk to her just one more time. Here, help me lift this pack onto my back, it's almost time to go. The rifle, too—no, it goes over the other shoulder; it's more comfortable to walk with it over there. Come on, give me a kiss for luck.

And do you know what my mother wrote back? She wrote that she loved me very dearly, and that I would always be her daughter, that her home was always my home, and the doors were always open. She told me I could come home whenever I wanted, but that I must understand one thing clearly. My brothers were still very young, and my father's knees were bad. If I came home, I would have to care for them and take care of the house. These would be my responsibilities, because if I came home, she would be going up to the mountains in my place.

Postscript

Most of the stories in this book were told to me during the period of 1985-1990. A lot has happened since then, much of it inspiring, some of it tragic. Here is an update, as of June 1, 1993, on the lives and deaths of the compañeros and compañeras in this book.

Anita is alive and well and feisty as ever. She continues her medical services to poor and underserved populations. Although her disfigurement makes her overly identifiable, and thus vulnerable, she is still with the URNG, although no longer in combat.

The old man lives on, still participating in his clandestine activities, still telling his wonderful stories to the new generation.

Lara was captured alive in 1991. She was tortured and kept in a pit, and subjected to two years of psychological abuse, and threats that if she attempted to escape, her family would be hunted down and killed.

She remains in captivity.

Sara and her *compa* left the mountains for awhile after he was badly wounded. While he recovered, she worked clandestinely on other projects. They have both returned to combat.

Jorge and Abram remain in the volcanoes, in active combat.

Everardo and I were married in 1991, one of the most mismatched yet happiest of couples. He vanished without a trace in March, 1992, during a brief battle. The army insists that he was wounded, and shot himself through the mouth to avoid capture. Yet no forensic confirmation was ever presented, and when I traveled to Guatemala for an exhumation, I was thrown out of the cemetery by the Attorney General and a large number of police. In early 1993 a young *compa* escaped from a military base and reported seeing Everardo chained to a bed for a number of weeks, and later undergoing torture. He and another witness also identified over thirty other prisoners being secretly held and abused by the army. The "Guatemala: Breaking the Silence" campaign is dedicated to rescuing the *compañeros* through political pressure, work with international agencies, boycotts, and efforts to impose trade sanctions.

Elena is working on a high school degree and is in charge of a houseful of recovering *compas*.

Gaspar struggles on, surviving the pain and the loss, his eyes firmly fixed on the other side of the Bridge. The memories of the fallen are with him at all times, giving him support, hope, and life.

Domingo and Fernando are dead. Domingo died in combat, shot through the head. Fernando was wounded and had to be evacuated from the mountains. Precious time was lost, and he died of gangrene.

Amelia was hit by shrapnel and came close to losing her leg. But she pulled through and is undergoing intensive medical care and therapy.

Camilo and Manuel struggle on, alive.

The priest of "Why and How" continues with the Church, sheltering the victims of the mad campaign of official terror still sweeping Guatemala.

Ruben is alive and has been joined in the

Postscript

mountains by his younger sister.

Lorena is alive, as is Lucia, who continues with her radio work.

Nicholas is alive, and waits for the day when he can see his son again.

The model villages continue as centers of military occupation and repression.

Tomas has been reassigned and fights on.

Martina and her small son are home in Guatemala. He has adapted effortlessly to his new life and is fluent in his Mayan dialect.

Bernardo was killed in the City.

Jorge Medico continues to care for the wounded.

La Voz Popular, after six years of heavy combat to silence its broadcasts, continues to be heard. Diego, who helped to found it, is alive but semi-blinded from combat injuries.

Dora is alive, but fell into a severe depression after the loss of her *compañero*. She is outside of the volcanoes, recovering with the help of the other *compas*.

Laura left the mountains, where the sounds of the explosions continued to traumatize her, and has taken up difficult and clandestine activities in another area. It was not necessary for her mother to go to the mountains in her place. A new generation of younger Guatemalans has made the difficult climb into the volcanoes, filling in the empty positions. The dead are replaced, but never forgotten.

As I write these lines, the battle for Guatemala rages on. Whether young or old, rich or poor, Maya or *ladino*, the people continue to struggle and resist, as they have, generation by generation, for the last five hundred years.

How You Can Make a Difference

If you assume that there's no hope, you guarantee that there will be no hope. If you assume that there is an instinct for human freedom, there are opportunities to change things, there's a chance you may contribute to making a better world. That's your choice.

—*Noam Chomsky*

Whether justice is possible in Guatemala depends in part on our ability to build grassroots movements to constrain a U.S. foreign policy which is bent on terror, torture, and murder aimed at "improving the investment climate." We must escalate the costs of the U.S. continuing that policy to the point where it is no longer worthwhile or feasible for our government to continue its support and training of those who rule Guatemala by force, hiding behind a veil of democracy. A wide range of activities over a long period of time is necessary, including: economic sanctions; medical care for the wounded; financing the peace talks; working to insure the safety of those combatants held captive by the Guatemalan army; and educating ourselves and others about the situation both here and in Guatemala.

Because the situation in Guatemala is changing rapidly, we suggest contacting a solidarity group in your area or one listed at the end of this section.

Actions can be as simple as getting friends to sign a petition or as involved as organizing a campaign of economic sanctions. The level of involvement is up to you.

Here are some examples of tasks already underway.

I. Economic Sanctions

In 1992 the US/Guatemala Labor Education Project organized strong boycotts against the Van Heusen company in Guatemala to force them to rehire workers who were allegedly discharged for attempting to unionize. The efforts were successful, and the workers rehired. Concerted actions are effective. For information on current boycotts call the Guatemala Project.

Economic sanctions are one of the strongest weapons we have in dealing with Guatemala. The death squads and the powers that be care very little about world opinion or political pressure. They care about money. That, after all, is what the war is about: the insistence of a tiny minority on keeping all the land and all the profits. We need to hit them where it hurts: in the pocketbook.

Economic sanctions had surprising impact in South Africa, and certainly would in Guatemala. We need to convince Congress to shut down all forms of economic aid. Perhaps most importantly, we need to shut down trade privileges. We don't need bananas, sugar, or coffee grown in a country that regularly murders its workers with such incredible rage and brutality. And we certainly should not be training their police or military forces.

Sanctions, as in any country, would have some

impact on the poor. However, the impact will be far greater on the rich, as the vast majority of profits go to the wealthy plantation owners. Cutting back profits will help force reforms, and ultimately save lives. To regain their privileges, all the authorities have to do is stop the killing and enact genuine human rights reforms.

II. Medical Care for the Wounded

In the United States it is not legal to actively support any military efforts of the URNG. However, strictly humanitarian aid is legal.

Lorena and her *compañero,* Tito, are down from the mountains after nearly a decade of fighting. They will never be able to return to combat because her foot is permanently damaged, and he is nearly blind. They were injured in a military bombing. They need medical care.

Because of injury many combatants will never be able to return to combat. Many have lost arms and legs or both; some have been blinded. Others have bones that will never mend, or injuries that will keep them from returning.

If you are a member of a church or civic or solidarity group that might be interested in "adopting" an injured *compañero* or *compañera,* and providing them with necessary surgeries, prosthetics, or other medical treatments, then write or call the Guatemala Project. We will send you information about the wounded and their needs, and tell you how to help these people, who have given so much, get healthy again.

III. Contributing to the Financial Cost of the Peace Talks

The peace negotiations between the URNG and the government continue. Despite long periods of inactivity and frustrating impasses, these talks are important. The longer the war, the more lives lost, of combatants and civilians alike. The peace talks must go on.

There are many costs involved in the negotiations process: air fares and hotels for participants, preparation of materials, communications. The URNG forces are an army of the poor.

If you would like to contribute to the peace talks, your assistance will be greatly appreciated and enormously useful. Send a check payable to "Guatemala Project: Peace Fund" at the address at the end of this section.

IV. "Guatemala: Breaking the Silence" about those held in prison camps

As explained earlier in this book, Comandante Everardo vanished in combat after seventeen years in the mountains. He and thirty other *compas* are being secretly detained and tortured by the Guatemalan army. They have been seen and identified by two escaped prisoners. The army insists that no secret prisons or prisoners exist. But this is untrue.

We are launching a campaign in this country to work with the United Nations, OAS, friendly foreign embassies, and members of the United States government to protest this situation and insist that the norms of the Geneva Convention and other international humanitarian laws be respected in this case.

There are numerous projects being prepared as part of this campaign, including intensive public education and mobilization efforts. Your help is needed to save these prisoners. Call the Guatemala Project for further information.

V. Educate Yourself and Others

Justice both here and in Guatemala depends on our ability to get information into as many hands as possible. For too long the *compañeros* and *compañeras* have been stereotyped as young hotheads from the City, filled with romantic notions about following in the steps of Che Guevara. As you can see, this shoe does not fit the Guatemalan foot. It's time to break the silence cloaking the realities of the country.

So tell your friends about this book and share it with them. Or give them a gift copy. All royalties go to the campaign to free Everardo and the thirty URNG prisoners of war. Get your friends thinking and talking about Guatemala. Get them to speak out and get involved.

Solidarity Groups

There are numerous solidarity offices in the United States which for many years have worked tirelessly for the people of Guatemala. They have fought for human rights, labor rights, freedom of the press and constitutional matters, and have long supported all civilian efforts for peaceful reforms. Unfortunately, there are far too many groups to list here. But the following organizations can help you locate the solidarity offices closest to you, and keep you informed about the ongoing situation.

How You Can Make a Difference

The Guatemalan Human Rights Commission/USA
3321 12th St NE
Washington, DC 20017   tel: 202-529-6599

Nisgua (Network in Solidarity with the People of Guatemala)
1500 Massachesetts Ave NW #241
Washington, DC 20005   tel: 202-223-6474

RUOG (Union of Representatives of the Guatemalan Opposition)
P.O. Box 3007
Grand Central Station
New York, NY 10163

Guatemala Support Network
4223 Richmond Ave #212
Houston, TX 77027   tel: 713-850-0441

US/Guatemala Labor Education Project
333 S. Ashland
Chicago, IL 60607 tel: 312-262-6602

The Guatemala Project
P.O. Box 650054
Austin, TX 78765 tel: 512-473-7149

Glossary

atole: local non-alcoholic drink made from corn.

campesino(a): Mayan or ladino peasant

Canjobal: One of the more than twenty dialects of the Mayan language still spoken in Guatemala,

comandante: commander

compa: abbreviated or familiar form of companero(a)

compañero(a): Literally friend or companion. In Latin America, the term frequently refers to a person who shares one's ideals. The guerrillas use the terms to refer to one another.

CUC: Campesino Unity Committee. A number of its early leaders, including the father of Rigoberta Menchu, were burned to death in the Spanish Embassy in 1981 when they peacefully occupied the building. They had sought to publicize the repression against the Mayan peoples.

EGP: Guerrilla Army of the Poor, one of the four revolutionary organizations comprising the URNG. Its base of operations is in the northwestern provinces of Guatemala, where it has carried out activities since the early 1970s.

Falda: Skirt. "Corte" is a word for Mayan style skirts worn by indigenous women in Guatemala.

FAR: The Revolutionary Armed Front. One of the four revolutionary organizations composing the URNG. The FAR operates mostly in the jungles of northeast Guatemala, and has been carrying out activities since the 1960s.

Finca: A plantation or farm.

Glossary

GAM: The Mutual Support Group for Families of the Disappeared, an organization founded in Guatemala in 1984.

Gringo: A person from the United States. The term is sometimes also used in reference to Canadians or Europeans.

Huipil: The embroidered or woven Mayan style blouse worn by indigenous women in Guatemala.

Indio: Literally, Indian. However, the term is used as a racist epithet, equivalent in terms of venom and hurtfulness to the word "nigger" in the United States.

Ladino: A Guatemalan of mixed heritage, with both Mayan and European ancestors. It may also include Mayan persons who have rejected their culture and assimilated to the European based culture in the towns and cities.

Mam: One of the more than twenty dialects of the Mayan language still spoken in Guatemala.

Mercado: Market place.

Marimba: Musical instrument much like a large xylophone, which is indigenous to Guatemala.

ORPA: The Revolutionary Organization of the People in Arms. This is one of the four revolutionary organizations comprising the URNG. ORPA operates mainly in southwest Guatemala, and began its activities in the early 1970s. However, in order to protect its fledgling structure and new members, it did not announce its existence until 1978, after some seven years of secret organizing efforts.

PGT: The Guatemalan Workers Party, one of the

four member organizations comprising the URNG. The PGT operates in the Guatemala City, where it has been carrying out activities since the 1950s.

Responsable: A member of the URNG forces who is responsible for a given project and group of compas. Such a person would be responsible for planning, security, training, and all activities.

Quiche: The name of a Guatemalan province, and also the name for the Mayan persons from that region. Quiche is the Mayan language of that region.

URNG: Guatemalan National Revolutionary Union. This is the united front composed of the four revolutionary organizations, including the EGP, FAR, ORPA, and the PGT. The URNG was formed in 1982.

Zone 12: A wealthy neighborhood in Guatemala City.

Reading List

If you want to learn more about the history and current situation of Guatemala, here are some additional sources. Citing a source in this list does not necessarily indicate complete agreement with the contents or analysis.

Jean-Marie Simon. *Guatemala: Eternal Spring, Eternal Tyranny* (Norton, 1987).

The text of this book is informative, but it is the photography that makes it invaluable. This is a very good "first" book about Guatemala because it does an excellent job of introducing the reader to the shocking mix of beauty and terror that defines life in Guatemala.

Elisabeth Burgos-Debray. *I, Rigoberta Menchu: An Indian Woman in Guatemala* (Verso, 1983).

Although Burgos-Debray did Menchu's story a disservice by failing to adequately order and edit her taped interviews, it is still a remarkable story. Rigoberta Menchu Tum, 1992 Nobel Peace Prize winner, comes through as an incredibly strong, determined, and resilient woman. A "must read" for its insight into the lives of the indigenous Mayan people in Guatemala.

Miguel Angel Asturias. *Men of Maize* (Routledge& Chapman, 1988; originally 1949) and *El Senor Presidente* (Macmillan, 1975; originally 1933).

These two political novels by Guatemala's first Nobel Laureate (for literature) show that the problems facing Guatemala, especially the virulent racism, are not new. *Men of Maize*, the first experiment in "magical realism," is a Latin American classic. Asturias's son, Rodrigo Asturias, is Comandante Gaspar Ilom, founder and leader of ORPA, who took his nom de guerre from the hero in *Men of Maize*.

Jim Handy. *Gift of the Devil* (South End Press, 1984).

A very informative and manageable history of Guatemala from pre-colonial times to the early 1980s.

Piero Gleijeses. *Shattered Hope: The Guatemalan Revolution and the United States, 1944-1954* (Princeton University Press, 1991).

Stephen Schlesinger & Stephen Kinzer. *Bitter Fruit* (Anchor Books/Doubleday, 1982).

Richard Immerman. *The CIA in Guatemala: The Foreign Policy of Intervention* (University of Texas Press, 1982).

All three of these books document the CIA-instigated and supported overthrow of democratically-elected President Jacobo Arbenz in 1954, ending Guatemala's decade of "revolution." This is a crucial period in recent Guatemalan history. Both *Bitter Fruit* and *Shattered Hope* make for very good, as well as informative, reading for anyone with even a slight interest in history. Gleijeses tells the story from the Guatemalan perspective by interviewing every living major player he could find. Although Arbenz died in exile in 1971, Gleijeses is apparently the only writer who has interviewed Arbenz's wife, Maria, who was a major influence on her husband's political and personal life.

Reading List

Americas Watch & Physicians for Human Rights. *Guatemala: Getting Away with Murder* (1991).

This report on the investigation (or lack thereof) of gross violations of human rights in Guatemala is a strong indictment of current and past abuses. It contains much detailed information about individual cases. Also, Americas Watch regularly publishes reports on human rights in Guatemala.

Susanne Jonas. *The Battle for Guatemala: Rebels, Death Squads, and U.S. Power* (Westview Press, 1991).

Jonas focuses on Guatemala since the CIA overthrow of Arbenz in 1954. She clearly knows Guatemala well, and her book is full of valuable information and analysis, but the academic writing style may discourage general readers.

Tom Barry. *Guatemala: A Country Guide* (Inter-Hemispheric Education Resource Center, 1992).

Barry's country guide is a good general reference. His concise overview of Guatemala contains sections on the economy, politics, the military, society, and foreign influence.

David Lindsey. *Body of Truth* (Doubleday, 1992).

Lindsey's novel is a gripping mystery that gives the reader a feel for life in the Guatemala City of today. Just remember that it is fiction and so uses literary license. The Spanish (though there is little of it) isn't very good, but the story is.

Alice Jay. *Persecution by Proxy: The Civil Patrols in Guatemala* (Robert F. Kennedy Center for Human Rights, 1993).

This human rights report is an up-to-date indictment of Guatemala's "voluntary" civil patrols. It contains detailed examples of the persecution and intimidation faced by those brave souls who refuse to serve.

Update
to the New Edition

1992 marked the 500th anniversary of Christopher Columbus' arrival in the western hemisphere. For the Indigenous peoples of the Americas this was less a matter of celebration than of commemoration of an ancient yet ongoing holocaust. The arrival of the Europeans brought them war, slavery, disenfranchisement, disease, the annihilation of their great civilizations, and the decimation of their populations. The compañeros and compañeras in Guatemala entered the New Year with high hopes, yet with a touch of foreboding. I heard many a wry joke to the effect that "The first time around was bad enough; we don't need any repeat performances."

For the U.R.N.G. that sense of foreboding turned out to be quite justified. Comandante Everardo returned to Guatemala to lead the Luis Ixmata frente, so long under his command, out of the mountains and into the countryside. An entirely new phase of the war was to begin, the first few months to play a crucial role. He vanished on March the 12th during a brief combat with the army near the Mexican border. Military leaders insisted that he had been wounded and killed himself in the battle to avoid being taken alive, and that they had buried his body in the nearby town of Retalhuleu. Nevertheless, his disappearance remained shrouded in contradictions and mystery.

Of all the promising young Mayans educated by

Gaspar Ilom and raised to the rank of Comandante, none were left alive. The younger ranking officers began intensive training. Jeremias, a favorite of everyone, wept for Everardo then returned to combat, only to be shot dead a few months later. A heroic compañera of many years was stabbed to death in the City. A key arsenal was lost. The peace talks disintegrated.

Throughout this terrible period, I traveled in and out of Mexico, frantic for news of Everardo, and frantic for my friends. I found them tired and saddened but bent on survival. Tragedy and hard times were no stranger to them. They just clung to one another even more tightly, spoke of the dead, and trained the newcomers. They continued to build the Bridge.

By the end of the year Amelia was carried out of the mountains with a leg shattered by an explosion. With her came her compañero, blinded in the same bombing. Amelia was told she must lose her leg. She declined. She was told she would never walk again. She gagged her way through calcium treatments and lifted weights between surgeries. A year and half later, I would watch her walking without so much as a limp. Don't ever tell Amelia what can't be done. I watched her and learned much.

As Christmas approached, the jokes began again, this time about escaping from those hellish days of 1992. Sure enough, the year ended with the news that Rigoberta Menchú had become the youngest recipient ever of the Nobel Peace prize. Santiago Cabrera Lopez escaped from Guatemala, reporting that Everardo and many others were alive and under torture. The battle for the prisoners of war began.

In the spring of 1993, President Serrano of Guatemala declared an "auto coup". President Clinton responded by cutting off all aid immediately. Shocked, the Guatemalan army had Serrano leave the country and tried to place his Vice President in power; an effort not accepted by the Guatemalan people. The Congress held a special election and placed the former human rights Ombudsman, Ramiro De Leon Carpio, in the presidency. He had been a good and courageous Ombudsman, and for a time there was hope that he could make a difference. That hope was cut short almost immediately.

De Leon Carpio's first act as President was to appoint General Enriquez from the more "moderate" factor as his new Minister of Defense. Evidently the rest of the army did not approve, for soon after, the President's cousin Jorge Carpio Nicolle, a prominent politician and newspaper editor, was assassinated, He was shot dead on a rural road near a military base by more than twenty masked men with military rifles saying "Get Carpio". The murder was immediately labeled "common crime" and ignored. Carpio Nicolle's widow and daughter inlaw carried out an extensive investigation on their own and found clear evidence of a military assassination. They were ignored, censored, threatened and defamed. The new human rights President remained silent, unable to even protect his own family members.

Within months, the Archbishop's office was announcing that human rights violations were actually increasing. De Leon Carpio slowly but surely reversed every human rights position he had ever held. When the civil patrollers shot into a crowd of people demonstrating against official abuses, the President hurried to defend the very PACs he had once criticized. When asked about secret prisons, he claimed that as human rights ombudsman, he had never seen any evidence of such prisons. Yet he, as Ombudsman, has investigated the case of the U.S. citizen Sister Dianna Ortiz, the nun who had been abducted. taken away in a police car, repeatedly raped, left with 111 cigarette burns on her back, and lowered into a pit filled with rats and dead bodies. It seemed that this case, among others, had slipped his mind. Not surprisingly, the human rights violations continued to rise sharply.

By late summer of 1993 I was able to return to Guatemala and open the grave where the army had claimed to have buried Everardo. Santiago had been telling the truth; I found the body of a completely different person, and my battle with the army was on.

In September I carried out a seven day hunger strike in front of the Polytechnica, insisting on a fair trial for Everardo and the other prisoners. I was the least exciting event that week, as the President attempted, unsuccessfully to oust corrupt members of the Congress, and the long suffering massacre survivors in the Resistance populations left their jungle hideouts and marched to the capital to demand recognition as civilians. As OAS was in town, investigating human rights abuses, this was a bit embarrassing, and the government insisted that the Populations were not being abused or bombed. Upon hearing this, the demonstrators simply dumped huge bomb and shrapnel fragments that had fallen on them for years and had been carefully collected as evidence, into the National Plaza. Army: Zero; Resistance Populations: One.

Meanwhile, another exhumation was being carried out, that of the Rio Negro massacre site. In the following months, we would all watch in horror as the bodies of 177 women and children would be pulled from a shallow trench not far from Rabinal. The men had left the village in the hopes that this would give some protection to their wives and children. Instead the army marched them all away, raping, hacking and strangling the women, smashing the children's heads against the stones. Those who survived began to work to build a memorial site for the dead, and soon began to receive the predictable death threats.

The war continued; with new compañeros and compañeras taking to the mountains and the frentes slowly recovering from 1992. The army alternately claimed that the U.R.N.G. had been virtually wiped out, but then again, that they were also still a very terrible threat. I watched in agony as one by one my old friends from the frente began to die; one committing suicide after a long and desperate run through the streets of a small town, another vanished, two more killed in combat. Others have taken their places, but for everyone else left alive, they are still present in the struggle.

The U.S. Embassy continued to hail De Leon Carpio as the great new human rights President, and to oppose the imposition of any sanctions. What was needed, the officials explained, was more institutional growth, more police to keep law and order against "common crime" and better "education" for the army. That the army should be out of power never appeared to enter into the possibilities.

In 1994 the peace talks began once again. A long and painful process of negotiations led, finally, to a human rights accord in March. It was a difficult period indeed, with enormous international pressure brought to bear on the U.R.N.G. to sign; and with neither the army, the companeros, or the civilians very happy with the results. The agreement required human rights to be honored, effective immediately, and for compliance to be monitored by a United Nations investigatory team. The army was furious. A Truth Commission was also provided for, to be established after the final cease fire under the amusing title of "Commission for Historical Clarification". Yet its powers were tightly reined in; for in reaching its conclusions, the commission could name no individuals in assigning guilt, only the army, or the U.R.N.G. Moreover, the Commission had no rights to prosecute, nor could evidence acquired by the Commission be used in later criminal trials. A poor person with little protection or ability to investigate could go to the Commission, and perhaps find out what the army had done, but no officers would be named, and the evidence could never be used in court. The civil rights groups were hardly pleased with this arrangement, believing that until consequences were attached to war crimes, such war crimes would continue. They wanted to say never again, but could not yet do so with any degree of certainty.

The army was equally distressed, and made its feelings plain enough. Human rights violations began to sharply increase. An eminent judge was assassinated, and a Congressman, shot the year before in a similar attempt, was shot again and re-hospitalized. Death threats began to proliferate once again against the leaders of the campesino organizations and human rights groups, and the disappearances and beatings were becoming more and more frequent.

Particularly distressing to the army was the thought of internationalists patrolling rural areas and finding out about the ongoing human rights abuses there. After all, the fiction of the new human rights President and the new and improved Guatemalan army were working quite well abroad. Something had to happen to keep people from talking to the foreigners, and that something certainly happened. Throughout the spring the rumors about foreigners kidnapping and selling Guatemalan children for their organs began to spread wildly in the countryside and some foreign women were attacked. One, June Weinstock, was so brutally beaten by a hysterical lynch mob that she spent months in a coma and has not fully recovered. These events all took place in rapid succession, in areas where the villagers, long famous for their gentle and hospitable ways, had never harmed anyone. Coincidence? I certainly think not.

The facts surrounding Ms. Weinstock's brutal beating are quite telling. The army was not far away, yet only arrived many hours later, after she had been severely injured. Part of the attack was actually filmed and some persons in the crowd were identified as being linked to the civil patrols and the army.

Distrust of foreigners had certainly been established, but this in the end had exactly the opposite effect of what the army had wanted. Human rights workers remained in the country, their long time relations with the campesinos quite unharmed. Instead, a travel advisory was clamped down by the U.S. Embassy, cutting off a key source of income for the upper class hotel and restaurant owners. There were immediate protests, complete with official declarations that these were merely isolated events, and that the country was indeed quite safe for tourists. The rumors began to die out as quickly as they had begun. There were no more attacks.

Meanwhile, the death toll for the Guatemalans rose higher and higher. The international community simply looked the other way. The United Nations team arrived months behind schedule, many people dying in the interim, without so much as a protest from the foreign governments. The Guatemalan military officers realized that they could do as they pleased, as long as they continued to sign agreements. No one in Washington would dare cut funding if they were still sitting at the peace table. Compliance would not be required of them. This assessment was quite accurate. The army continued to kill and their international funding continued to arrive.

Interestingly, Vice President Gore was in Central America in early 1994 pressing for regional trade plans and discussing future extensions of NAFTA for the central american nations. Guatemala, of course, could not be included until a final peace accord was signed, and the State Department began, during this time frame, to push mightily for a prompt agreement. No comments were made as to compliance, No sanctions were even threatened.

By late 1994, the Guatemalan civilians were utterly disillusioned with the peace process, noting, correctly enough, that the army was just signing papers while the civilians continued to be murdered. The breach of public confidence proved fatal to the process, which began to disintegrate by late fall. It was only by frantic UN intervention that the talks were able to continue in 1995.

Meanwhile, my own relationship with the U.S. Embassy began to sour during this same time period. Throughout 1994 it was made clear to me no steps were going to be taken other than "mentioning" the matter with less and less vehemence, to the army. All priority was going to the peace process and my case was clearly in the way. I finally reached a complete dead end, and began my hunger strike in the National Plaza, demanding that Everardo be given a fair trial, in October 1994. The Embassy showed great concern but did little to resolve the case until "60 Minutes" revealed that the CIA had sent a memo to the Embassy confirming that Everardo had indeed been captured alive by the army in 1992. On the 31st day of my strike, the U.S. Ambassador issued a demarche, or formal diplomatic statement, to De Leon Carpio, stating that Everardo had indeed been captured alive, that he had been lightly but not seriously wounded, and that he had been a prisoner for at least a number of weeks, after which time nothing else was known. I halted my strike on day 32 and returned to Washington to speak with Anthony Lake, National Security Advisor to the President.

During my last days in the Square, a storm had been gathering over the proposed increase in the bus fares. Once again, the memory of those massacred in the bus strike of long ago caused tempers to boil over and the people took to the streets, burning buses and protesting the increase. As usual, the security forces responded with remarkable brutality. A young woman accompanying me during the strike saw police fire into a crowd of unarmed people, and watched them crumple in bloody piles onto the pavement. That evening, as I packed my bags, I could hear the crackling of automatic rifles outside, while on television scenes of beatings and arrests at the University flickered across the screen.

Washington, of course, helped me not at all. By January our government had sent the National Guard to Guatemala and I was told that sanctions of any kind were simply out of the question. I asked for the files on my case and received nothing.

Throughout the winter the violations were becoming ever more severe in Guatemala. Once again, the ethnic rights group CERJ began to lose members to the death squads. A Belgian priest was killed near his church. More than fifty people were murdered, many showing signs of torture, between January and March alone. No one knows how many died in the more remote rural areas. The plaque for the Rio Negro massacre site was found smashed. The survivors continue under threats.

On March 12, 1995 I resumed by hunger strike, this time in front of the White House. After twelve days, Representative Toricelli met with me and informed me that Everardo was indeed dead, and been ordered executed by Col. Alpírez in 1992.

Moreover, Alpírez was a CIA contact, and had ordered the death of U.S. citizen Michael Devine in 1990. In the ensuing scandal, it was also discovered that the CIA had continued covert military aid to the Guatemalan army, even though it had been cut by the U.S. government after Devine's murder.

As I finish this post script, Gaspar Ilom faces some of the most difficult decisions of his life. Should a peace agreement be signed? If signed will it be enforceable? Have they gained enough ground to attempt civilian reforms once again? Or should they remain at war? Some thirty-five years have gone by, but another generation can indeed go to the mountains, and are ready and willing. But should he send them? If they climb the volcano, many will die. But if they don't, will more live? The army is weak and highly exposed, but like a great wounded beast, still very dangerous. Peace could work. But is the international community going to make it work? Or will the errors of 1994 be repeated, with the foreigners looking the other way as the Guatemalans continue to die in the streets. Will we help them with this army that we ourselves created, put in power, trained and funded all these years? Or must the compañeros and compañeras continue to battle their way to the other side of the Bridge? What is our answer?

Jennifer Harbury
May 1995